Extending Professional Contributions

Edited by Tim Murphey

Professional Development in Language Education Series, Volume 2

Tim Murphey, Series Editor

Teachers of English to Speakers of Other Languages, Inc.

Typeset in Giovanni and Bunky
by Capitol Communication Systems, Inc., Crofton, Maryland USA
Printed by Kirby Lithographic Company, Inc., Arlington, Virginia USA

Teachers of English to Speakers of Other Languages, Inc.
700 South Washington Street, Suite 200
Alexandria, Virginia 22314 USA
Tel 703-836-0774 • Fax 703-836-6447 • E-mail info@tesol.org • http://www.tesol.org/

Director of Publishing: Paul G. Gibbs
Managing Editor: Marilyn Kupetz
Copy Editor: Ellen Garshick
Cover Design: Capitol Communication Systems, Inc.

ISBN 1931185107
Library of Congress Control No. 2002116676

Contents

Series Editor's Preface

TESOL's Professional Development in Language Education series was conceived by the TESOL Publications Committee as a way to provide a wide array of choices to teachers for continuing their development throughout their careers. The series is based on the recognition that those who contribute most to the profession and to their students' learning see their own continual learning and development as crucial to their work. Such professionals regularly challenge their beliefs, their methods, and the status quo; they seek out and explore a variety of ways to teach and learn. In doing so they not only contribute to their own professional development, but also create a contagious wave of excitement that entrains colleagues and communities of learners.

Professional development is the raison d'être of professional associations like TESOL, and thus we need to think more consciously about how we do it and challenge ourselves to seek better and more effective ways to develop ourselves. Besides making efforts to improve themselves and their students, TESOL professionals also seek to stimulate the profession and give back to the field. All the contributors to this series are sharing in this effort by offering insightful and innovative ways of professional development.

Volume 1 in the series, *Becoming Contributing Professionals,* is focused on what new teachers can do to continue their development. It seeks to inspire them to build on the excitement of initial education and incorporate continual development into their lives. A common thread in all three volumes, started here, is that technology can play a significant role in TESOL professionals' continual development.

Volume 2, *Extending Professional Contributions,* highlights midcareer professionals and looks at ways they have sought to continue developing. Most apparent in this volume is the amount of development that comes from collaboration with other teachers and researchers. Professional development is immensely richer when done with others in a community in which excitement and ideas grow exponentially with colleagues.

Volume 3, *Sustaining Professionalism,* looks at ways that more seasoned professionals have continued to develop professionally. Many of these chapters reveal how personal lives are intertwined with professional lives and how many professional decisions have major consequences for life histories, taking us to new places and giving us profound experiences. It is gratifying to see how we as TESOL professionals can continue to innovate and rise to challenges throughout our careers.

These three volumes are testimony to the diversity and courage in the TESOL profession. Although the contents of the three volumes flow across the different stages of a career in TESOL, all TESOL professionals can learn from many of the chapters in each volume and can learn how to stimulate the professional development of their colleagues. I am excited to think of the impact this series will have on many teachers and the continual quality of TESOL as it offers professional development globally.

Tim Murphey

Acknowledgments

Thanks to Karen Johnson (past chair of the TESOL Publications Committee), Marilyn Kupetz (managing editor), and the TESOL Publications Committee for great leadership and vision; to the TESOL editorial staff, Ellen F. Garshick and team, for superb copy-editing and flexibility; to Joy Egbert (editor of Volume 1) and Pat Byrd and Gayle Nelson (editors of Volume 3), for being so enthusiastic about this project and making the volumes so connected; and to the contributors to this volume, who were amazingly eager and prompt with deadlines. Finally, thanks to my editor father, Walter Hubert Murphey, who turned 91 shortly before Volumes 1–3 went to press and inspired me more than he will ever know—*ton fils*.

Introduction

Tim Murphey

Sing silence into symphony
Paint pale into vivid
Write pen into heart
And Dance
     imagination
    in the wind

—Tanak Akay

This is an exciting book. Cutting to the chase, the message is that anything can be. You as a TESOL professional can overcome isolation in most any institution or in a foreign culture. You can collaborate with your colleagues next door, across the city or state, or in another country. You can collaborate with the students in your classes. You can write journals about your researching and teaching, or even go back to graduate school. You can stay home, live where you like, and teach courses over distance. You can explore computer-assisted ways to learn that allow students to collaborate and even do electronic MA portfolios, professionally developing yourselves along the way. If you really wanted to, you could volunteer to teach overseas for a short time and have the adventure of your life. Or you might stay where you are and gather enthusiastic teachers around you to form a group of explorers. To get the word out, you could even write about these things and create publications for others to write in. And the word is, "Participation precedes learning" (Bateson, 1994, p. 41): Just do it!

As I edited this volume, I found myself wanting to immediately try out the suggestions in each chapter. The contributors offer novel perspectives on how to go about professional development with energy and insight. Their contributions fall into three areas: Collaborating and Researching, Using Technology, and Volunteering and Inviting Professional Development.

Collaborating and Researching

The first six contributions deal mainly with collaborative development and research. In chapter 1, Janzen and Beck, who found themselves partially isolated in their separate institutions, describe a long-distance collaboration on research concerning a writing course that culminated in professional presentations and publications, and, of course, their own development as teachers and researchers. Field and Nagai (chapter 2), a native and nonnative English speaker, respectively, complement each other's perspectives and develop themselves as they seek to ecologically change their colleagues' perspectives on the teaching of reading in a Japanese university. Also in Japan, Stewart and Lokon (chapter 3), another native/nonnative pair, team teach a class and find they can collaborate with their students to revise the course and develop their professional knowledge. Gorsuch and Beglar (chapter 4) collaboratively innovate using a distant interviewing process to gather valuable information and analyze their first time teaching a graduate-level course in second language acquisition. Next, Borg (chapter 5) describes keeping personal research journals as an insightful way to develop while teaching and to use when writing up research for publication, thus collaborating with one's prior reflecting selves. In chapter 6, longtime teacher Miller describes her brave decision to return to graduate school to do her PhD—a collaborative research move par excellence—and gives valuable advice to those contemplating such a move.

Using Technology

The next three chapters describe how you as a TESOL professional can use technology to stretch the limits of professional development for yourself and those you teach. Green (chapter 7) recounts her switch to teaching distance courses over the Internet, a move she made to be able to choose where she lived and spend more time with her children. Pawan and Jacobson (chapter 8) complement Green's contribution with a description of their online courses at their university and the ways they stimulate participants to intensively interact and collaborate with each other, learning much from their students in the process. Shaver, Hart, and Avalos (chapter 9) created an innovative electronic portfolio assessment for MA students that ecologically can be used to document and encourage continual professional development even after the MA course ends.

Volunteering and Inviting Professional Development

The last three chapters deal with ways to develop professionally by giving expertise to others and inviting others to join you. In chapter 10, Carbery and Croker describe their volunteer work as teacher educators in Thailand and its effect on their professional lives. Sato (chapter 11) tells how he started a local professional development group among like-minded high school teachers in Japan and how they stimulate development among themselves. Chapter 12 describes the creation of publications for teachers to contribute to, with narratives by Murphey, Connolly, McLaughlin, Churchill, Schwartz, and Krajka. This last piece suggests that, besides writing for publications, you can greatly enhance your own professional development by creating and editing publications ranging from departmental newsletters and university research journals to online journals.

The contributors to this volume, who come from many parts of the world, show how you as a TESOL professional can collaborate, use technology, create professional development groups, publish, volunteer, take risks, make a new life, and in the process change yourself and the world. When you are a TESOL professional, you can make almost anything happen!

Reference

Bateson, M. (1994). *Peripheral visions.* New York: HarperCollins.

Contributor

Tim Murphey has studied and taught in Florida (MA), Switzerland (PhD), Taiwan, and Japan (where he now teaches at Dokkyo University). He is currently applying sociocultural theory to learning and teaching, teacher education, and alternative learning forms.

1 Long-Distance Collaboration: Rescuing Each Other From the Desert Island

Angela Beck and Joy Janzen

Narrative

"Are there any questions?" As hands begin to rise around the conference room, we share a sigh of relief and a smile. Our presentation on strategy instruction in writing at the TESOL convention has gone smoothly, and traveling the long path that led us here has been worth all our effort.

Joint presentations are common at TESOL conventions, but most presenters have the luxury of working at the same place or at least living nearby. Our situation is very different. Not only do we live and work in distant states, but we also have little contact with other TESOL professionals in our daily lives. Our solution to these problems has been to collaborate on a long-term research program. This work has kept us fresh professionally as teachers and teacher educators, and it has helped us become part of a wider community.

Joy
As a newly minted university professor, I found it a distinct adjustment to move from a well-populated doctoral

program to a school in which I was the only specialist in applied linguistics and TESOL. It was, and continues to be, an isolating experience. From the start, however, I was determined to continue my professional development as best I could by reading, doing research, and making connections with colleagues.

One of the responsibilities in my new job was to teach a course in freshman composition for nonnative speakers of English. I had mixed emotions about teaching a composition class. Still, I struggle with composition classes more than with any others I have ever taught. Becoming a good writer is a long-term process that many students find difficult and discouraging. Teaching writing means asking myself endless questions about how to balance instruction in organization, language, process, and content effectively—and I am never satisfied with my answers. Moreover, the difficulties I anticipated in teaching writing could not be made easier by comparing notes with other teachers working with ESL students at my school because mine would be the only ESL composition class. However, I love working with ESL students, and I would have limited contact with them in the rest of my work.

Then I got the idea of calling for help.

Angela

When Joy first called me, I had recently accepted a position as an instructor in an extension program in teacher education. I was teaching at various off-site campuses, and, like Joy, I felt isolated. I rarely had the opportunity to meet with fellow instructors, and many of them specialized in disciplines other than applied linguistics. Furthermore, although my primary interest is in composition, my new duties gave me limited opportunities to teach writing, so I had fewer chances than I wished to use my past experiences in teaching and research.

At first, the discussions Joy and I had focused on my methods for teaching strategic planning in writing, but gradually we developed the idea of collaborative research, which would have several benefits. Through collaboration, Joy would be able to think about the class in a productive way by focusing on some research questions. I could contribute knowledge about the teaching of writing and suggestions for measuring changes in student metacognition. I would also have the chance to take a more active role in writing research. Together, we would continue to increase our understanding of metacognitive behaviors while engaging in the professional discussion neither of us had access to at our current positions.

Description

Discussions of teacher research have become more and more frequent in the TESOL field since the early 1990s (Allwright, 1997; Burns, 1996; Wallace, 1998), and these discussions have suggested many benefits for teachers' examinations of their own classrooms. Teachers can focus on local issues and contexts, which will answer their particular questions about instruction and learning. They can reflect productively on what they observe, which can lead to improved teaching practice. Despite these benefits, teacher research can be very difficult to implement effectively. Teachers may lack sufficient distance from their students or classroom interactions to identify effective means of researching the questions they want to answer. They may also lack experience or background in reliable research techniques. Even if they begin a promising project, teacher-researchers sometimes abandon data gathering or analysis simply because they are overwhelmed by instructional demands.

One solution to these dilemmas is for teachers to make connections through long-distance collaboration, in which each partner can inform a project with unique knowledge and perspectives. Collaboration may help isolated members of TESOL become more active, and, when a project leads to some form of sharing with a wider community, the field can benefit by hearing from new voices with different points of view (Flowerdew, 2000; Hafernik, Messerschmitt, & Vandrick, 1997).

Steps

We outline the following steps as a straightforward progression, but the process is in fact recursive. Completing one set of tasks may require setting new goals, and sharing research results may lead to setting goals for a new project. For example, as part of our research, we measured students' use of writing strategies before and after a semester of instruction to see if they had acquired a greater understanding of planning and metacognition. This ongoing research informs how one of us (Joy) teaches her composition classes, and we continue to refine our research questions and gather new types of data, processes that may lead to further conference presentations or publications.

1. Develop connections. Attend conferences, become a member of a professional or advocacy group, and join school associations. Look up previous contacts, such as fellow students, professors, or peers at an earlier job site.

2. Identify colleagues who share your interests but have different experiences or backgrounds that can inform your viewpoint.

3. Identify questions, procedures, and goals for your collaboration. These areas are the crux of any research project. Teachers are often interested in broad issues that are complex and therefore difficult to measure. Research collaborators can help each other locate a measurable question to investigate and, perhaps, identify existing measures to use. Starting with limited questions and procedures helps keep the research process on track and makes it more likely that you will actually finish your project.

   Matching your research questions to the evidence you gather depends, in part, on your long-term goal for sharing the results of the project. For example, if you want to give an in-service workshop to fellow teachers, you may simply discuss a method you are trying out and recount what you have noticed informally in the classroom. However, if you want to convince others in a published article that your teaching approach is effective, you will need more rigorous evidence of change or development. As you think about questions, procedures, and goals, consider the following points:

   • What do you want to discover about your classroom or students? For example, what question do you have about your students' behavior? What teaching approach do you want to investigate?

- How will you measure student behavior? For example, how can you show that your teaching has affected the students' understanding? How will you identify the particular aspects of language or content that students are struggling with?
- How much time do you have to gather material? How much material do you need?
- Can you use readily available information, such as student assignments, or do you need to develop new means of gathering data?
- Do you need oral or written data? If you want oral data, how will you gather them? How will you transcribe them? How will you analyze them?

4. Set up the tasks to fulfill these goals, and assign responsibilities. This is clearly an ongoing process, as your goals or tasks are unlikely to remain identical over the course of the collaboration. Ours certainly did not. At some point, however, preferably early on in your collaboration, consider in detail what each person's expectations are. For example, we decided to divide the data we were focusing on, and then we reviewed each other's analysis. When we wrote a conference paper, we also divided the writing responsibilities, assigning separate sections to each person, and then combined our efforts.

5. Keep in touch. Decide which member of the collaboration team will be responsible for keeping the others on task and in touch, and how often contact should be made. We cannot emphasize enough how important it is to share your work with each other as the project progresses. Do not let your fellow collaborator(s) fade away, or the project will fade with it.

6. Be flexible and open. Flexibility in collaboration means constant discussion and compromise. You will sometimes need to respond to a collaborator who has different ideas or priorities than you do. Make the process as painless as possible, with all partners considering whether they are really negotiating a compromise or demanding that their ideas be used. If differences are not easily resolvable, consider the goals you began with. What did you want to accomplish? Why? If you

have changed your goals or means, why have you done so? We are very much aware of the value of our partner's contributions to joint work, and we are willing to defer to each other's expertise. We also have different strengths, in terms of both knowledge of the field and approaches to teaching writing and metacognition. To keep our collaboration running smoothly, we follow several routines. In writing materials together, we pass drafts back and forth and mark the changes we make in boldface to draw the other's attention to them. We also write questions in the drafts for the other to answer. Just as crucially, we supplement our e-mailing with telephone calls to ensure that neither person feels slighted or underappreciated.

7. Find ways—through presentations, Web sites, and publication—to share the results of your project with others. Sometimes, multiple ways of sharing might present themselves; we have taken our findings to several conferences and have submitted them for publication. Keep in mind that long-distance collaboration is about connections and professional engagement, and finding ways to share your work increases your opportunities to connect. We have met new colleagues and gained different perspectives on our work through the very process of dissemination. As you think about the best ways to disseminate your results, consider the following issues:

- What aspects of your findings are relevant to researchers, teacher educators, administrators, or fellow practitioners?

- How can your findings be adapted to different audiences?

- Many researchers feel that they have finished a project with more questions than answers. How can these questions be framed and disseminated so that they, too, add to the knowledge of the professional community?

8. Reflect. How does this collaborative relationship fuel your professional development? How does it increase your understanding of your teaching? Of your students? Of language? How has this relationship led to greater professional and personal fulfillment? Has it helped you become a model of

what you ask your students to do (e.g., work productively in groups, investigate language behavior, and become more aware of learning or writing processes)? Consider the future as well. What problems did you encounter? How can you overcome them next time? Can there be a next project? For us, this chapter grew out of the success of our convention presentation, and we have worked on other publications separately and together as a result of ongoing research.

9. Repeat.

Conclusion

Through collaborative research, you can engage in those practices that TESOL professionals value: inclusion, cooperation, participation, respect, inquiry, and self-reflection (Birch, Toll, & Voitus, 2000; Edge, 1996). For one of us (Joy), this research has been a productive means of self-reflection in particular. She has gained greater insight into students' perceptions of writing and of students' writing behavior. As a teacher educator, research also gives her face validity in talking to future teachers about teaching writing and classroom research. The other (Angela) has found that geographic isolation does not mean that her voice will go unheard, and, through collaboration, she has discovered the means to further examine her teaching approaches and testing instruments.

In encouraging others to try collaboration, we are reminded of experiences we have had as teacher educators. We regularly encounter innovative teachers who express doubt about whether or how they can contribute to the sum of professional knowledge. If collaborative research can help new voices be heard, then all of us in TESOL will benefit. Research and collaboration are not easy paths; they take time, effort, and patience. But through collaboration, we can connect with others, and we are not left to struggle on alone.

Resources

Allwright, D. (1997). Quality and sustainability in teacher-research. *TESOL Quarterly, 31*, 368–370.

Allwright argues that teacher research may be valuable if it functions as exploratory practice, that is, as a search for local understandings rather than for incontrovertible findings and universalistic theory.

Birch, B., Toll, M., & Voitus, A. (2000). Building community among personnel in an intensive English program. *TESOL Matters, 10*(3), 17.

Burns, A. (1996). Collaborative research and curriculum change in the Australian Adult Migrant English Program. *TESOL Quarterly, 30*, 591–605.

Burns describes the policy and curricular changes in the Adult Migrant English Program, which were based in no small part on the teacher research undertaken by 30 teachers and four curriculum coordinators. Although the process of collaboration is not described in detail, the positive outcomes of long-distance collaboration are highlighted.

Edge, J. (1996). Cross-cultural paradoxes in a profession of values. *TESOL Quarterly, 30*, 9–30.

Edge outlines various conflicts and paradoxes TESOL professionals experience. He argues that the TESOL profession embraces the values of inquiry, pluralism, and cooperation.

Flowerdew, J. (2000). Discourse community, legitimate peripheral participation, and the nonnative-English-speaking scholar. *TESOL Quarterly, 34*, 127–150.

Flowerdew traces the attempts of a nonnative-English-speaking scholar from Hong Kong to publish an article in a refereed journal. In so doing, he explores the notion of peripheral participation in one profession.

Hafernik, J. J., Messerschmitt, D. S., & Vandrick, S. (1997). Collaborative research: Why and how? *Educational Researcher, 26*(9), 31–35.

The authors discuss the benefits of carrying out long-term collaborative research as well as some of the mechanisms that make collaboration effective.

Wallace, M. J. (1998). *Action research for language teachers.* Cambridge: Cambridge University Press.

This book outlines the benefits of teacher research, offers suggestions for designing and implementing research projects, and gives several sample projects.

Contributors

Angela Beck (beckae0@erau.edu) is an assistant professor of humanities/communications and general education programs coordinator at Embry-Riddle Aeronautical University (ERAU), in the United States. She heads the development of ERAU's fledgling literacy-across-the-curriculum program. Her research interests include interdisciplinary collaboration, genre-based instruction, and theories of expertise in writing.

Joy Janzen (janzen@mnstate.edu) is an assistant professor in the English Department at Minnesota State University, Moorhead, in the United States, and she directs the ESL licensure program for future K–12 teachers. Her research interests include the development of students as strategic readers and writers.

2 The "Dead Hand" Project: Intercultural Collaboration and Professional Development

Mary Lee Field and Noriko Nagai

Narrative (Mary Lee) _____

Many years ago, I took an undergraduate teacher education course at a state university. I was not particularly interested in the course. After all, what could that older teacher have to say to me? Actually, she said something that has resonated throughout my 42-year teaching career.

"What influences our teaching the most?" asked the professor. It seemed a silly question. Surely, I could teach any way I wanted. "The way we were taught before," the professor announced, "the dead hand of the past." I scoffed at this idea. It could not apply to me. However, after many years of teaching, I see that I have repeatedly engaged in the slow and sometimes painful process of removing that "dead hand" grasping my shoulder.

Rather recently, I was describing this image to my Japanese colleague, Noriko, at a Japanese university where we were both teaching. We discussed how the influence of the past applied to Japanese teachers in particular. In fact, I had visited a Japanese teacher's reading class, where students spent 90 minutes hunched over a three-page

English text, referring frequently to bilingual dictionaries, reading two or three sentences aloud at a time, and then translating each sentence word by word. Although the teacher had earned a PhD in the United States, his method of teaching was the time-honored intensive reading technique I had seen 25 years ago in Japan. Moreover, during those 25 years, the Japanese Ministry of Education has repeatedly urged reforms in methods of teaching English.

As Noriko and I talked, we realized we were in a unique position to design and implement a project concerning reading. We knew we could learn from each other, share our information with other Japanese teachers, engage others in a discussion of teaching reading, and possibly plant seeds for change. Our collaboration, between a foreign teacher and a home-country teacher, was facilitated by our more than 20 years' acquaintance and mutual fascination with the teaching of reading. Eventually, this collaboration would make a strong contribution not only to the professional development of the faculty but also to us.

Description

Professional development is a new concept in many national Japanese universities, including ours. Although an occasional expert might visit the campus and give a lecture, no group on campus or in any college or department is responsible for thinking about, planning, or implementing a professional development program. Teaching is tightly guarded as each professor's individual territory. Classes are rarely opened to other teachers. There is no precedent for faculty's discussing curriculum, sharing course syllabi, or establishing goals or outcomes. We were facing uncharted terrain.

In Japan, as in many other countries, university professors are hired according to their specializations, not for their ability to teach those specializations. Moreover, there were various cultural barriers to overcome, including the fact that (a) no one (except the two of us) wanted any changes, (b) it is totally inappropriate for a foreign teacher to impose what Freeman (2000) calls *imported theory* on local knowledge, and (c) it was inappropriate for a younger Japanese teacher to lead a committee that included older colleagues.

On the more positive side, our individual strengths and abilities were remarkably complementary. One of us (Mary Lee), the U.S. teacher, had had a long-term interest in teaching reading; the other (Noriko), a Japanese teacher who received her PhD in the United States and had studied and taught there, was feeling dismayed and discouraged by the reading levels of her Japanese students. The American wanted to learn more about cultural factors that influence the teaching of reading in Japan, actual classroom practices in Japanese universities, and Japanese beliefs about teaching and learning. The Japanese teacher wanted to learn more about methods of teaching reading, reading theory, and professional development techniques useful for our university. By working with Noriko, Mary Lee was allowed access to the resources of the university otherwise inaccessible to her because of her limited Japanese speaking ability. By working with Mary Lee, Noriko was able to add the weight of an older and higher ranking colleague to the project. Although rank and age were not important in our cooperation, these factors count heavily among Japanese professors.

First, we wrote a grant proposal (in Japanese but with input from both of us) to address the teaching of reading in our English curriculum. We received a modest sum of money from the department, enough for some books, a scanner, occasional technical help, and incidental expenses. There was, alas, no reduction in our teaching loads. International collaboration and professional development did not make us candidates for any type of reward from the university. We were definitely working in the real world.

We defined our goal, at first rather lightheartedly, as lifting the "dead hand of the past" from our colleagues' shoulders. More specifically, the project focused on lowering the affective filter so that Japanese teachers would be willing to listen to the foreign teacher's imported theory and feel free to reflect on their own practices, goals, and methods. Basically, we tried to devise a nonthreatening way to encourage participants to think about teaching English reading by raising their awareness of reading processes in their native language. Our project included the following:

1. a series of meetings with faculty members teaching a reading course called English Practicum

2. materials for the teachers (in Japanese and English) as a kind of text for raising awareness of reading processes

3. presentations in English, but most discussions in Japanese, as the teachers were discussing their own classes and their ideas about reading

4. consciousness-raising about the mental processes involved in reading both in the L1 and in the L2

5. contrast and comparison between how the faculty participants had been taught in the past and were currently teaching

6. identification of the many goals and methods that apply to the teaching of reading

We had no specific goals for change or reform. Instead, we wanted to make the professors aware of reading processes and alternative goals and methods. The desire to make changes would have to come from within each teacher. When (and if) that happened, we planned to show videos of teaching, analyze different reading textbooks, invite teachers to our classes, and discuss specific lesson plans for reading classes.

Steps

Setting goals and planning the steps for a professional development project takes considerable time. Although we tried to plan all the details from the first step to the conclusion, our plans had to be adjusted at several points as the project was implemented. Thus, flexibility is also a critical element. The following steps serve as a guide to constructing this type of project.

Identifying the Situation, the Need, and the People

1. Time your project carefully. TESOL professionals may often see situations in need of change. However, the appropriateness and timeliness of change is a delicate issue. For example, making changes in small areas of curriculum design at the same time as major nationwide, education ministry–mandated reforms were being discussed in national universities was not a good idea. There was not enough energy for fighting on many fronts.

2. Choose a project that grows from real needs perceived by and important to a wider group. Low scores on the reading section of the Test of English as a Foreign Language (TOEFL) or Test of English as an International Language (TOEIC) may indicate a situation needing to be remedied, but do the students and other teachers agree?

3. Talk with each other about how you like to work, what your time constraints are, how you feel about correction and input, and how to handle disagreement. Collaborative projects depend on people's ability to communicate and work together. However, cultural differences may make collaborative projects difficult or even impossible.

Identifying the Challenges

4. Explore the cultural barriers that may have an impact on the collaborative project you propose. For example, if teachers have no precedent for discussing course syllabi and planning a curriculum together, how can you introduce those tasks in your project? If the home-country professors are hesitant or shy about speaking English, should the discussions be in their native language? If age, rank, and other status markers are important in the culture you are working in, how can you be sure not to violate some of those values?

5. Set goals for the project according to the situation, not according to your own notions and expectations. None of the teachers in our group wanted changes. We knew they would only change from inside. We could not and did not impose goals for change on the group.

6. Consider carefully the backgrounds, assumptions, and interests of the people in your group. Foreign teachers need to read and understand as much as possible about the home-country culture. For those in the Japanese context, Rohlen and LeTendre's *Teaching and Learning in Japan* (1999) is the most thorough and balanced resource that we found. None of our teachers was trained in methods of teaching English. We could not expect them to be conversant with EFL teaching theory, second language acquisition theory, or EFL methodology.

Consequently, we began with discussions about reading in their native language and the nature of L1 reading processes. In other words, change needs to be ecological and scaffolded from the participants' positions.

Organizing the Project

You must be acutely aware of the difficulty and delicacy of a project that may challenge ingrained habits and deeply rooted beliefs about ways of teaching and learning. In planning the parts of the project, build in as many ways as you can to lower the affective filter.

1. Conduct meetings (or parts of meetings) in the home-country language.

2. Avoid giving rules and mandating changes.

3. Although it is not easy, identify and eliminate invasive, top-down, directive, or intrusive elements in your plans.

4. Begin where the participants are in terms of ideas, training, background, and beliefs about learning and teaching.

5. Make meetings as interactive as possible, and give participants tasks to complete that challenge their assumptions.

Conclusion

The benefits of collaborative projects are many. Foreign and home-country teachers will enrich each others' understanding of theory and of home-country practice. The participants in our workshops felt that they benefited from their first-ever discussions of their classes. This project led us to give several presentations at professional meetings and to undertake a much larger collaborative project (underway at this writing) involving more faculty, more students, and a major university program. Our collaboration has taught us how to cooperate better, how to engage more faculty members to work with us, and how to structure more ambitious tasks.

We cannot claim success in terms of major changes in the teaching of reading at our university. However, we did not think that major changes could, realistically, happen in such a short period of time. The dead hand clutches tightly. Indeed, for older teachers, especially those close to retirement, there will be no changes. Nevertheless, we are pleased that some younger teachers have begun to talk about reading a bit differently, and we think that gradual, internal changes are beginning to occur. Most of all, we are satisfied that a dialogue has begun, that it did not lead to rancor, that it led to other projects, and that cooperation and cross-cultural exchange were possible. Now, professional development is not such a new concept at our university.

Resources

Freeman, D. (2000, October/November). Imported theories/local understandings: Part 1. *TESOL Matters*, 1, 6.

Freeman, D. (2001, January/February). Imported theories/local understandings: Part 2. *TESOL Matters*, 5.

Anyone teaching abroad and engaged in professional development projects with home-country teachers will appreciate this article. It is a shortened version of Freeman's plenary address at the 34th Annual TESOL Convention in 2000, in Vancouver, British Columbia, Canada. Collision between local understanding and imported theory can torpedo even the best project, and Freeman provides information to help avoid those crashes.

James, P. (2001). *Teachers in action: Tasks for in-service language teacher education and development*. Cambridge: Cambridge University Press.

Although this book mainly addresses teacher education, chapter 2, "Exploring Teachers' Knowledge," is packed with exercises, questions, information, and procedures that are applicable or adaptable to professional development contexts.

Richards, J. C., & Lockhart, C. (1994). *Reflective teaching in second language classrooms*. Cambridge: Cambridge University Press.

The exercises in this text provide a variety of ways to get teachers thinking and talking in nonconfrontational ways. Much of the material here is easily adaptable to professional development programs.

Rohlen, T. P., & LeTendre, G. K. (Eds.). (1999). *Teaching and learning in Japan*. New York: Cambridge University Press.

This collection of essays analyzes the major beliefs, assumptions, and practices concerning teaching and learning in Japan. The cumulative effect of the articles is both wide and deep. These essays stimulated frequent discussions between us as we struggled to understand the features and complexities of the specifically Japanese "dead hand."

Contributors

Mary Lee Field (maryleefield@earthlink.net) is coauthor of *From Reader to Reading Teacher* and the outgoing book review editor for *TESOL Journal.* From 2000 to 2002 she taught at Ibaraki University in Mito, Japan. This teaching experience, her second in Japan, was greatly enhanced by this professional development project with her former student, Noriko Nagai.

Noriko Nagai (nagai@mx.ibaraki.ac.jp), a professor at Ibaraki University, has a PhD from the University of Michigan and taught at Duke University from 1985 to 1993. She conducts research in the field of utterance comprehension mechanisms within the framework of relevance theory.

3 Professional Development Through Student and Teacher Reflection Journals

Timothy Stewart and Elizabeth Lokon

Narrative

We are not Lucille Ball and Desi Arnaz, but our differences are as pronounced. We taught a cross-cultural communication course together for the first time and worked across various boundaries. One of us (Tim) is a Canadian male and a veteran English language teaching faculty member at a small liberal arts college in Japan. The other (Elizabeth) is an Indonesian female who had been newly hired to teach cross-cultural communication. Whereas Lucy and Desi used their differences to create comic moments on television, we used ours to gain insights into our effectiveness as team teachers in a fully integrated cross-cultural communication course. We planned, taught, and reflected together.

Employing a content-based language teaching approach, we aimed to integrate the teaching and learning of discipline-specific content and language objectives as seamlessly as possible. To analyze our own practices, we wrote journal entries evaluating the tasks in the course. We then discussed the contents of these journals, thus creating rich multilayered and multiperspectival data for reflective analysis.

Description

According to Sandholtz (2000), teachers see collaboration as a vital part of professional development. When in need of advice, teachers usually seek out other teachers rather than administrators or outside experts. One of the most intimate approaches to collaboration is team teaching. This chapter describes a case of reflective team teaching aimed at improving course design. However, the main benefit, we discovered, came not so much from collaborating with another teacher but from collaborating with our students. Although we encourage teachers to reflect collaboratively, we suggest that teachers miss a valuable opportunity for their own development and that of their students if they do not include their students in the reflective process.

In reflective teaching, teachers assess the purposes of their practice, reflect on the classroom consequences of their action, and find more effective means of achieving their ends. In this approach to professional development, teachers "collect data about teaching, examine their attitudes, beliefs, assumptions and teaching practices, and use the information obtained as a basis for critical reflection about teaching" (Richards & Lockhart, 1994, p. 1). Yet, although this reflection-in-action process can provide teachers with invaluable knowledge, the learners' perspective is often missing. This gap is problematic because studies indicate a possible mismatch between the perceptions of teachers and those of their learners (e.g., Block, 1996). We used journals to better understand students' perspectives and how they learned.

We—the co-teachers—and 38 students wrote eight journal entries each over one 16-week teaching term. We wrote immediately after a specific task was completed. These tasks were primarily concerned with meaning, were related to the world outside the classroom, focused on task completion, and were assessed in terms of task outcome. Thus, our definition of *task* follows that proposed by Skehan (1996).

In recording language learning or teaching experiences, one must write regularly and candidly. Journals have to be "analyzed for recurring patterns or salient events" (Bailey, 1990, p. 215). We did this analysis after the semester as we redesigned the course for the following year.

Steps

Preparing for Journal Writing

1. Find reflection partners. The first set of partners in this process is your students. The second partner is another teacher. Candidates include a team-teaching partner, a teacher who teaches another section of the same course, a master teacher assigned to mentor your professional development process, or a trusted colleague.

2. Decide on the purpose of reflection. Understand clearly why you are going through the collaborative reflection process and what you are trying to accomplish through it. Articulate the rationale and goals clearly to all reflection partners.

3. Write up the questions. Collaboratively, decide on the set of questions for everyone to reflect on. The students may or may not be involved. The advantage of involving them at this early stage is to establish a democratic learning community that increases everyone's stake in the reflection process. However, designing the questions takes less time if only the two teachers do so. We designed the following questions without students' input:

   - Were you absent for part of this activity? (yes or no)

   - What did you learn from this activity?

   - How much did you learn in this activity? (Rate on a scale of 1–4, where 1 is *very little* and 4 is *very much*.)

   - Explain your answer for the above rating.

We asked the above questions because we were designing a brand-new course and team teaching it for the first time. Our primary objective was to discover the appropriateness of the activities in the course. You may want to ask a different set of questions that better fit your situation and goals.

Writing the Journal

4. Have both teachers and students respond to the same set of questions so that triangulation is possible. (Obviously, the colleague who responds needs to have watched or participated in the lessons.) Use the same set of questions several times throughout the course to allow for multiple reflections.

5. Make sure students understand the purpose of the process. Make clear to them that the reflection is for your professional development, not to grade their understanding or mastery of the material. With questions asking for a rating, such as *How much did you learn in this activity?*, some students may be inclined to give themselves a high mark to show you that they have understood the materials when, in fact, they have not. It is therefore critical to state explicitly that you are interested in their honest opinions so that you can improve your teaching.

6. To prevent confounding effects, do not allow participants to read each other's journal entries until after they have written their own.

Reflecting on the Journal Entries

7. Decide on the timing for the reflection. There are two basic ways to time the reflection process: (a) collect all journal entries at the end of the semester and reflect on them all, or (b) read and reflect throughout the semester. Each approach has advantages and disadvantages. Using the first approach, as we did, you can assure students that what they write will not have any bearing on their grade. This might inspire them to write more candidly. On the other hand, you cannot use the benefit gained from the reflective process until the next time you teach the course.

   Reflecting on the journal entries throughout the semester enables students to experience changes as the course unfolds. This in turn may motivate them to write more in subsequent entries. However, some students may be inhibited from writing frankly by the fear of having their grades affected by the contents of their journals. Of course, you can easily address this concern by making the entries anonymous, but you may still recognize students' handwriting. When to conduct the reflective process depends a lot on the culture of the classroom and the relationships between teachers and students.

8. Do the reflection. The following steps can be done without face-to-face contact:

   - You read your colleague's journal entry. Your colleague reads yours.
   - You reflect and write a response to your colleague's entry while he or she does the same.
   - You and your colleague read each other's responses.
   - You and your colleague independently read the students' journal entries, noting ideas that neither of you included in your entries.

   The following steps require face-to-face contact:

   - With your colleague, discuss all of the above. End the discussion with a specific set of changes that you plan to make.
   - If students are involved actively in the reflective process, report these changes and new ideas to them, and have them respond.
   - After reviewing students' responses to your ideas for change, make concrete plans to implement changes.

Learning From the Reflection

At first we thought that the entries would be so similar that there would not be much to reflect on. As we systematically analyzed the entries, however, it became clear that much could be learned from these journals to improve the course.

9. Pay attention to both process and content learning. We, the course instructors, were nearly exclusively focused on skills and processes, whereas students were more concerned about issues of content learning. For example, when we reflected on an ethnographic research project on particular restaurants, many students wrote that they had learned about Japanese society

and culture change. Others stressed becoming more aware of their own actions and unconscious assumptions. We, on the other hand, made comments about various qualitative research skills that were gained or needed further development. The contrast between our journal entries and students' along this process/content line continued throughout the semester. By analyzing students' journals, we realized that we tended to focus our attention on process learning, whereas students focused theirs more on content learning. We—teachers and students—should be more aware of both types of learning in the future.

10. Remember that the full scope of learning may not always be obvious. Students were keenly aware of their personal development throughout the course. We saw some of this development but not the full scope. Students wrote about gaining skills and confidence by doing the research projects and presentations; the development of cooperative learning skills was another major theme in student journals. Some commented that they had learned a great deal from each other. The message in these comments is that our students felt empowered by the classroom dynamic. The fact that students found the class conducive to learning and to personal growth beyond the explicitly stated set of course objectives was very encouraging for us as we revised the course.

11. Improve task design and teaching based on students' comments. Six (four males and two females) out of 38 students commented at different times that a particular task was too difficult. Not surprisingly, all of these comments concerned tasks that asked students to apply the concepts learned in the course. We need to consider what in our design or teaching of these tasks would cause 50% of the eight males in the course, but only 2% of the females, to make such comments. The fact that most of our male students had lower English proficiency than our female students may have been a factor here. This suggests a deeper question about the relationship between English language study and gender.

12. Consider what students do not write about. One of us (Tim), as the English language teaching specialist, was struck by the sparseness of comments in student journals on language learning. This raises questions regarding the nature of language and content learning in discipline-based courses. The course tasks were all designed to focus on meaning, although discrete language skills were taught throughout. Even though students indicated in their course evaluations that they had learned to think in new and different ways, they may have wanted more explicit language instruction. Or they may have been learning a lot of language in the course but simply were not aware of it. Maybe we could include some methods for the students to realize their own improvement in English in future courses.

13. Take note of the students' view of relevance. Unlike our journal entries, the students' entries repeatedly emphasized the usefulness of tasks for studying abroad. The semester of study abroad has a particular significance in the minds of our second-year students. Before going abroad, students gauge the relevance and value of all learning in terms of whether it will be useful for their upcoming semester abroad. When students voluntarily and consistently state that the tasks are useful for study abroad, we can be sure that, overall, they have learned what they want to know. To further validate the course content, we would like to find out eventually if they have the same positive comments about the course's relevance when they return from their study abroad.

Conclusion

Using journals for teacher development is a labor-intensive process, but by reflecting on our journals we learned a great deal from differences in our perspectives, particularly the differences between our journals and the students'. Systematic analysis and reflection on the journals revealed our strengths and weaknesses.

Despite our surface differences, we learned that, as instructors, we wrote reflection journals that were quite similar. This came as a surprise to us and brought us closer to one another. Despite the similarities in our journals, we learned a lot from this collaborative writing process. The ongoing process of trying to articulate our reactions to tasks brought forth our own assumptions and expectations. The journals gave us a forum to explore further and deeper not only each other's but also our own teaching philosophies, taken-for-granted beliefs, and hidden agendas. Exploring this kind of knowledge with colleagues is essential for professional development. It also steered us toward improvements in future versions of the course.

We would not have learned as much from a quantitative evaluation at the end of the course. We believe that as a result of this reflection process we have a better understanding of ourselves as teachers, a clearer focus on our learning objectives for the course, and a stronger teaching partnership. We also believe that students in future courses will benefit from improvements that we plan to make. Finally, we believe that continuous reflection and dialogue among teachers and students in a course are essential for improving the effectiveness of classroom activities.

As we reflect on our initial metaphor, we suspect that Lucy and Desi developed their flawless performances over time through a lot of behind-the-scenes dialogue and reflection, gaining sensitivity to their audience. We feel that increasing this sensitivity is critical in our professional development and that writing reflection journals with students can help us become better teachers.

Resources

Bailey, K. M. (1990). The use of diary studies in teacher education programs. In J. C. Richards & D. Nunan (Eds.), *Second language teacher education* (pp. 215–226). New York: Cambridge University Press.

This volume also includes a good chapter on teacher development through reflective teaching by Bartlett.

Block, D. (1996). A window on the classroom: Classroom events viewed from different angles. In K. M. Bailey & D. Nunan (Eds.), *Voices from the language classroom: Qualitative research in second language education* (pp. 168–194). Cambridge: Cambridge University Press.

Burton, J., & Carroll, M. (Eds.). (2001). *Journal writing*. Alexandria, VA: TESOL.

This book, part of the Case Studies in TESOL series, gives ideas on journals for teachers and students.

Matsuda, P. K. (1999/2000, December/January). Teacher development through native speaker–nonnative speaker collaboration. *TESOL Matters, 1*, 10. Retrieved December 16, 2002, from http://www.tesol.org/pubs/articles/1999/tm9912-03.html

Murphey, T. (1993). Why don't teachers learn what learners learn? Taking the guesswork out with action logging. *Forum, 31*(1), 6–12. Retrieved December 16, 2002, from http://exchanges.state.gov/forum/vols/vol31/no1/p6.htm

Richards, J. C., & Lockhart, C. (1994). *Reflective teaching in second language classrooms*. Cambridge: Cambridge University Press.

Sandholtz, J. H. (2000). Interdisciplinary team teaching as a form of professional development. *Teacher Education Quarterly, 27*(3), 39–54.

Skehan, P. (1996). A framework for the implementation of task-based instruction. *Applied Linguistics, 17*, 38–62.

Vermont Center for the Book. (n.d.). *Reflective journals*. Retrieved December 16, 2002, from http://www.vermontbook.org/action-research8.html

Contributors

Elizabeth Lokon (elokon@miyazaki-mic.ac.jp) teaches cross-cultural communication and EFL courses at Miyazaki International College, in Japan.

Tim Stewart (tstewart@miyazaki-mic.ac.jp) has team taught courses since 1989 and now reflects on his teaching at Miyazaki International College.

4 Fostering Graduate School Teacher Development Through Peer Interviewing

Greta Gorsuch and David Beglar

Narrative

This story starts at a conference in Vancouver, British Columbia, Canada, in 1999. One of us (David) was attending from Japan, and the other (Greta) was attending from Texas, in the United States, where she had taken a job after leaving Japan 6 months before. We knew each other quite well but had never before met. Besides both being longtime language teachers in Japan, we had graduated from the same doctoral program. Although David's cohort met in Osaka and Greta's met in Tokyo, we had many of the same instructors.

During our conversations in Vancouver, we learned that we had both recently started teaching graduate-level applied linguistics courses after many years of teaching EFL. Further, we learned that we were both a third of the way through our first semester of teaching second language acquisition (SLA) courses. We agreed that, of all the new courses we had been teaching, SLA presented singular challenges. These challenges were at times painful, but they made us realize clearly that we were in the midst of a shift in our teaching careers and that this shift entailed very different kinds of thinking, planning, and knowledge use. It was a confusing yet exhilarating time, and we felt the need to make sense of it.

We formulated a plan. We wanted to capture the growth and change that was taking place in our teaching in a way that would allow us to express our thoughts in detail as the course was unfolding and permit us to exchange this information over distance. Most important, we wanted to more clearly discern significant patterns in our thinking, patterns that might reveal useful specifics on improving our teaching of this conceptually difficult course. We decided that multiple exchanges in the form of written peer interviews during and after the semester best fit our needs. The concept of exchange is important here, not in the sense that we wanted to prescribe solutions for each other, but in the sense that we wanted to describe our concerns and the types of activities our students were engaged in and use our reading of each other's accounts to attain greater clarity. We found that even simple questions such as *What did you mean by that?* helped us notice new facets of a complex situation and express a new understanding more precisely. This exchange resulted in a body of data that were rich, detailed, and clearly stated. In addition, setting ourselves the same questions, answering them, exchanging our answers, asking each other to clarify statements, rethinking our answers, and then analyzing our accounts after the semester was over helped us identify routes for improving our teaching of SLA. Moreover, we learned that our experiences were not unusual for teachers teaching in new content areas.

Description

The use of peer interviews as a means of reflection and growth is not new. Many observers in general education comment that self-reflection is an effective means to enhance teacher development (e.g., Zeichner, 1999). Our report here is an account of reciprocal interviews as a means to self-reflection and, as such, is an embodiment of a view of research in which "the beliefs, cognitions, attitudes, and decision making processes of the teachers themselves" (Widdowson, 1997, p. 125) are of primary importance. We wanted to develop ourselves as teachers of SLA, as we believed SLA was an important and compelling field of study and as we would likely be asked to teach it repeatedly during our careers. However, although we each had taught several semesters of graduate-level language testing and teaching methodology courses, we agreed that the SLA courses presented extraordinary teaching challenges. Several reasons may account for this. First, the field of SLA has grown exponentially in recent years and has become difficult for even experienced faculty to comprehend. Second, growth in SLA has meant a diversification of the field, making problematic the decision on what topics to include in a course. Third, SLA, despite being a subject offered in 75% of U.S. TESOL and applied linguistics MA and PhD programs listed in the American Association of Applied Linguistics' (2000) directory, does not readily welcome newcomers. Students in our classes found the academic prose of SLA research studies and textbooks conceptually opaque. As a result, in terms of day-to-day teaching, we frequently had to construct and articulate impromptu, student-attuned interpretations of the materials in our courses. One final reason we found SLA so daunting to teach is that SLA courses have a less intuitively obvious pedagogy than other language teacher education courses do.

We believe that using peer interviews takes on added importance in higher education teaching contexts, as such contexts rarely provide new faculty with opportunities for development. This problem is compounded by the fact that faculty preparation and learning are treated as afterthoughts in higher education (Dinerman, Feldman, & Ello, 1999), a practice that results in a prevailing attitude at universities that simply having a doctorate is a license to teach (Eison & Stevens, 1994). Unfortunately, earning the degree may not adequately prepare faculty for the demanding instructional tasks that lie ahead. Typically, university faculty learn to be faculty by being graduate students and completing a doctoral degree. The student-as-teacher-apprentice is a familiar concept to educationists writing of teaching in general (Lortie, 1975) and of TESOL teaching in particular (Freeman, 1994). However, although student experiences can provide powerful surface images of what teaching looks like, they cannot give insights into the many decisions graduate faculty make in applying what they know about TESOL or applied linguistics content to classroom tasks, discussions, or lectures primarily because most graduate students are thinking about mastery of the course content, not reflection on their teachers' pedagogical decisions. During doctoral studies, students soon learn that "grades and achievements in the cognitive domain tend to be emphasized" and that "teaching skills are downplayed or missed" (Richlin, 1994, p. 256).

Complicating the situation is the reality that skilled teaching in one area of content does not necessarily translate into skilled teaching in another (Shulman, 1987). In other words, although our EFL teaching experiences (more than 30 years between us) may have developed what Berliner (1991) terms *pedagogic knowledge* (generalized knowledge about classrooms, activities, and students), it cannot be assumed that these experiences adequately prepared us for teaching applied linguistics courses. As a result, we began our long-distance, collegial efforts to mutually reflect on our teaching of SLA courses through peer interviews based on our belief that university faculty are themselves ultimately responsible for their own learning. We recommend the technique we outline below for any teachers who find themselves teaching new courses and who wish to intensify their development.

Steps

1. Generate interview questions. The term *peer interviews* should not imply a series of casual chats between colleagues. For the procedure to have relevance to the issues you are concerned with, you will need to work out beforehand the general questions that will guide the interviews. During our initial planning in Vancouver, we agreed on three general questions:

   • What challenges are we facing in teaching SLA for the first time?

   • How are we responding to these challenges?

   • Can our experiences be explained in terms of a model of pedagogical reasoning?

   We used the first two questions to generate more specific questions, and a log that one of us (Greta) had been keeping from the first weeks of the course also suggested questions. Here are some examples: *During the first few class meetings, what feelings did you have? What situations arose?* and *When you first learned you were going to teach the course, what did you do?*

2. Read other sources on teacher development and learning, and come to an understanding of the issues being discussed. Our third general question was essential in that we sought to apply a model of pedagogical reasoning to our accounts. We surmised that our growth in teaching would follow the same general pattern as other teachers', and we wanted to ensure that our development and learning would not be a closed circuit. Rather, we wanted our experiences to have relevance to the ongoing scholarly conversation concerning the development of content- and situation-specific teaching skills in general education (e.g., Korthagen & Kessels, 1999) and in TESOL teacher education (Richards, 1998). We learned through our reading, for example, that content-specific teaching knowledge is thought to develop through experience and that one of the hallmarks of this knowledge is an understanding of how to adapt materials and activities to specific student levels and interests (Shulman, 1987).

   Our reading had two other benefits: First, we were able to generate additional questions that later turned out to be essential in capturing and explaining our growth. For instance, we asked, *Did you have any sort of image of your teaching before you actually started teaching the course? Did it change over time?* and *How did you deal with special features of your students?* The second benefit was that we had access to a model with explanatory power that we could use to analyze our accounts.

3. Review the questions. Once you have formulated a set of questions, both participants should review them. Delete questions that have no relevance to your general questions, and add others that are aligned with them. You may wish to ask a colleague to conduct an external audit of the specific questions by outlining your general questions and asking the auditor whether the specific questions appear relevant.

4. Conduct the peer interviews. We found that it is important to give ourselves time to answer the questions and not assume that a first attempt at answering is sufficient. After answering

the questions, put them down for at least a week. Then return to them and add details. One of us (Greta) found that keeping a pre- and post-SLA class meeting log helped in answering the questions.

5. Exchange, comment on, and return the interview data. One of us (David) wrote his comments and questions to the other (Greta) on strips of paper and stapled them to her interview data before sending them back to her. Greta then answered each question and integrated the answers into the interview data.

6. Analyze the data. By the time you reach this stage, the term *interview data* will likely mean a 10- to 15-page document for each interview participant—a great deal of data in prose form. Although you will probably learn a great deal simply by answering the interview questions and answering each other's comments and requests for clarification, we strongly urge you to analyze your data. As you read both sets of data, identify larger themes. Make a list of the themes, and arrange specific texts from the data under those themes. In our case, we typed specific texts into a word-processing program, printed them out, cut them apart, and rearranged them according to the themes that we had identified. This technique allowed us to identify multiple themes within the scope of each of our three general questions.

The benefits of the peer interviews were enormous for us, for a number of reasons. We learned that our knowledge of SLA could not automatically be applied to teaching it. We also concluded that our experiences of learning SLA at the MA and PhD level did not adequately prepare us to teach. We further learned that our experiences in this respect were not unique in university teaching and that our instinct to take responsibility for helping ourselves through peer interviewing was correct. In addition, we learned that students' background and motivation were important factors affecting our feelings of frustration and success in teaching SLA. We believe that our accounts of our initial concerns and later insights into adjusting the readings, in-class activities, and assignments to specific student attributes provide confirmatory evidence of Shulman's (1987) model of pedagogical reasoning development in teachers. Most importantly, we discovered specific routes to improving our teaching of SLA.

One of us (Greta) learned that she needed to further develop her critical comprehension of SLA content, meaning that she had to comprehend SLA texts and research papers she planned to assign for student reading from multiple points of view. She also learned that planning her syllabus by assigning topics to specific class meetings at the outset would more effectively enable her to prepare for classes. The other (David) discovered that he had gaps in specific areas of his SLA knowledge, and he committed himself to reading intensively in those areas. Moreover, he came to understand the need to engage students in data analysis and discussion activities. Finally, we both learned that the traditional end-of-semester literature review assignments were not the best way to capture students' understanding of SLA content and their ability to synthesize and apply that content. Shorter, more focused, and more frequent assignments seemed more suitable. We believe we could not have learned these things with such depth and specificity without the peer interviews. As a final step, we encourage you to write and publish a report of your findings (e.g., Gorsuch & Beglar, 2002) so as to share your knowledge with other interested members of the education community.

Conclusion

Whatever preparation previous MA- or PhD-level course work gives for teaching specific courses in the future, we believe that it is ultimately the responsibility of individual teachers to make efforts to develop themselves and to strive toward providing increasingly valuable instruction. The process of conducting our peer interviews, analyzing our data, and striving to relate our experiences to the broadest possible research context was essential to making sense of our experiences teaching SLA for the first time. This process was significant in moving us forward in our professional careers and helping us sustain our growth.

Resources

American Association of Applied Linguistics. (2000). *North American graduate degree programs in—or related to—applied linguistics*. Eagan, MN: Author.

Berliner, D. C. (1991). Educational psychology and pedagogical expertise. *Educational Psychologist, 26*, 145–155.

Dinerman, M., Feldman, P., & Ello, L. (1999). Preparing practitioners for the professorate. *Journal of Social Work, 18*, 23–32.

> The authors make clear the role of doctoral study and early university faculty teaching experiences in the ultimate long-term development of teaching excellence in universities. Most doctoral-level faculty seem unaware of their own roles as preparers of future university faculty (their doctoral students) in that they do not overtly discuss the design of graduate-level courses.

Eison, J., & Stevens, E. (1994). Faculty development workshops and institutes. In W. A. Wright (Ed.), *Teaching improvement practices: Successful strategies for higher education* (pp. 206–236). Bolton, MA: Anker.

Freeman, D. (1994). Knowing into doing: Teacher education and the problem of transfer. In D. C. Li, D. Mahoney, & J. C. Richards (Eds.), *Exploring second language teacher development* (pp. 1–20). Hong Kong: City Polytechnic of Hong Kong.

Gorsuch, G., & Beglar, D. (2002). *Teaching graduate second language acquisition courses: Views from new faculty.* Unpublished manuscript.

Korthagen, F. A. J., & Kessels, J. P. A. M. (1999). Linking theory and practice: Changing the pedagogy of teacher education. *Educational Researcher, 28*(4), 4–17.

> The authors comment on how teachers' theoretical knowledge becomes practice. They note that "in order to learn anything during teacher education, student teachers must have personal concerns about teaching or they must have encountered concrete problems" (p. 5).

Lortie, D. (1975). *Schoolteacher: A sociological study.* Chicago: University of Chicago Press.

Richards, J. C. (1998). *Beyond training.* Cambridge: Cambridge University Press.

> In this significant book for teacher educators, the author outlines the state of current graduate TESOL and applied linguistics teacher preparation programs. While the courses promote the design of

pair learning, cooperative learning, communicative tasks, and so on for ESL learners, the graduate faculty in the programs do not themselves employ these alternative methods of teaching.

Richlin, L. (1994). Preparing the faculty of the future how to teach. In W. A. Wright (Ed.), *Teaching improvement practices: Successful strategies for higher education* (pp. 255–282). Bolton, MA: Anker.

Shulman, L. S. (1987). Knowledge and teaching: Foundations of the new reform. *Harvard Educational Review, 57*(1), 1–22.

This article is much cited among foremost teacher educators in TESOL, and for good reason. The author sets out in clear, accessible prose a likely model for explaining and predicting teacher development.

Widdowson, H. (1997). Approaches to second language teacher education. In R. T. Tucker & D. Corson (Eds.), *Encyclopedia of education: Vol. 4. Second language education* (pp. 121–129). Boston: Kluwer Academic.

Zeichner, K. (1999). The new scholarship in teacher education. *Educational Researcher, 28*(9), 4–15.

Contributors

Greta Gorsuch (greta.gorsuch@ttu.edu) is an assistant professor of applied linguistics at Texas Tech University, in the United States. She is interested in language testing, educational policy, and teacher education.

David Beglar (david_beglar@kmug.org) teaches graduate level applied linguistics courses at Temple University Japan, Osaka and Fukuoka. He is interested in vocabulary acquisition, language testing, and teacher education.

5 Pulp Fiction?
The Research Journal and Professional Development

Simon Borg

Narrative

Over the last two days I haven't been feeling at all good about the work. I realise I've been a bit misguided in the direction I've invested effort in over the last few months. I've tried to write papers without having done enough analysis of my data; I've focused not just on one teacher, but on a part of that teacher's data, and in doing so I've lost sight of the larger picture. I read the data for teacher 1 yesterday and I can see that what I've written so far gives a simplistic picture of this teacher's work. The analysis is extremely thorough, but I fell into the novice researcher's trap of getting so excited about writing and publishing that I've selected data that gives a neat picture of things and ignored anything that tends to make it messy. Now I can see this is a contradiction in terms for any qualitative researcher, because the reality I am investigating is messy, and it is not my job to explain away that messiness but to attempt to present it and to understand whether there are systematic patterns of thinking and behaviour underlying it. That's what my research is all about. So my decision here as I move on is to stop writing and to continue analysing. The research is all about the data, and I've yet to obtain a holistic picture of what the data are telling me.

I'm not saying all the reading I've been doing hasn't helped. But for now I can put all my articles aside, and study the data. I need to find out what themes the data hold, because they might suggest avenues of reading I haven't thought of yet.

I guess this is a kind of a turning point in my work. I've become aware that I had developed a distorted view of what my work is all about. It's not about reading papers, it's not about one teacher's use of grammar activities. It's a lot deeper than that. I know I've got good data that have the potential to tell us something about teachers' work in the classroom. It's just a question of me getting rid of this misguided desire to publish and to focus on the really rewarding task that faces me, that of coming to terms with my data. I know that there will be plenty of time to write when the work has been done, and that at that stage I can base my writing on a thorough analysis of the whole picture rather than on a narrow assessment of part of the data.

So today I start on the data for teacher 2. Good luck. I'm glad I've realised things weren't going well and that it was my fault only that they weren't.

Description

The extract above comes from a journal I kept during the course of a research project. This journal made a significant contribution to my thinking and development during the project, and my aim here is to outline ways in which this occurred. I also give some suggestions based on my experience for keeping and using a journal as part of the research process.

Much has been written about the role that reflective writing—diaries and journals—plays in teachers' professional growth (e.g. Bailey, 1990; Francis, 1995; Hoover, 1994; Numrich, 1996). The collective message emerging from this work is that reflective writing can give much insight into the personal and often implicit processes that teachers experience in their work and development, and that these written accounts have significant benefits for the writer. In broad terms, by documenting and reflecting on their experience, writers benefit from an enhanced awareness of themselves as people and as professionals, an awareness that makes for more informed professional decision making (Holly, 1989a).

Little has been written, though, about the use of diaries and journals as a form of reflective writing that researchers engage in during a project and through which they document their personal experience of the research process (Janesick, 1999, is an exception here). Such writing is sometimes referred to as a *research journal* (Thomas, 1995), and here I discuss, with reference to my own experience, the contributions such reflective writing can make to professional development of individuals engaged in research in TESOL.

Steps

In terms of format, many options for keeping a research journal exist (e.g. lists, letters, dialogues, or narratives, all of which can be typed or handwritten), and given the personal nature of journal writing, an important part of the process is for you to define a format that best suits you. My journals are written as narratives in the first and second person, and I word-process my entries. More central than issues of format to using a journal effectively, however, are the quality and content of the thinking and writing that shapes the journal, and here I list some suggestions with respect to these.

1. Write and review regularly. Effective journal writing is a sustained process over a period of time in which you make and review (i.e., read and think about) entries regularly. It is important for you to maintain contact with the journal so that it becomes a narrative that is an integral part of the research process.

2. Engage in open discussion with yourself. The audience for the journal is the writer, not others, something that is clearly illustrated in my extract above. Writing journals with others in mind (e.g., editing and polishing the prose) may interfere with

the kind of reflective writing that will make the journal most beneficial. Writing to yourself also allows you to do so with greater openness and honesty.

3. Use the journal as an archive. Keeping a record of events, experiences, and thoughts in the journal allows it to become what one teacher in Holly (1989b) calls "a great pulp memory bank" (p. 6), a record of the research process that can play a key role in enhancing your understanding of it.

4. Write spontaneously and freely. Holly (1989b) quotes Ferrucci (1982):

> If we start by writing freely about the issue that concerns us, we will find ourselves expressing things not previously thought of. We have to formulate explicitly that which we feel implicitly, thereby clarifying to ourselves what may have been a confused morass. In this process we may also come to new conclusions and ideas about courses of action to take . . . . We should not be surprised that unconscious material surfaces so readily in our writing . . . . Writing stimulates this interchange and allows us to observe, direct, and understand it. (pp. 75–76)

5. Reflect and explore. Despite its value as an archive, the research journal is much more than a record of events, and the narrative presented above illustrates the centrality in the journal of reflecting on and exploring ideas by writing about them. The entry was prompted by strong feelings of uncertainty about the value of my work, and I turned to my journal to examine this situation and to try to understand the root of the problem. I started by stating the motivation for the entry, then describing the nature of the problem and considering what I had done wrong. I then articulated my new awareness and understanding of the problem, and made a brief statement of the action I needed to take. In the final part of the entry I acknowledged the importance of the realization I had made, restated where I had gone wrong, reminded myself what I needed to do, and reassured myself that there would be time for writing—more effective writing—later on. I was not simply recording my thoughts here; they were developing as I wrote.

In terms of the benefits of keeping a research journal, my experience highlights two broad categories of benefit: those which stem from the process of writing itself (process benefits) and those which derive from the retrospective analysis of the record that the journal constitutes (product benefits). I have described these in detail elsewhere (Borg, 2001) and summarize them here.

My experience suggests that the very process itself of writing a research journal was beneficial in many ways. The writing process

- assisted me in articulating and rationalizing concerns and exploring solutions

- gave me an outlet for acknowledging, expressing, and examining feelings

- was a key way of establishing goals, formulating plans, and deciding on actions

- was central to the processes of describing and evaluating my progress (or lack of it)

- enhanced my attempts to clarify concepts and their implications for the research

- was a fundamental way of discovering, capturing, exploring, and pursuing ideas

- played a central role in structuring what generally started off as chaotic thoughts

I also benefited a great deal through retrospective analyses of what I had written. As a documentary archive, the research journal was beneficial to my understanding of the research process. The journal

- served as a reminder of past ideas and events, which guided subsequent action

- provided a record of plans and achievements, which facilitated evaluation

- supplied an account of events and procedures, which allowed a more detailed writeup of the study

- allowed me to recall the thinking behind key decisions in my work

- constituted an instructive narrative of my professional growth

- served as physical evidence of progress, which gave me a sense of achievement and motivated me

- provided an account of experiences and ideas that, when returned to, often sparked further insights

The product benefits I have described here stem from the manner in which the journal is a permanent account of many aspects of the research process that can be returned to at any time. This database of experience greatly enhances the researcher's ability to make informed decisions about the research process, provides a global picture of patterns and themes in the researcher's work and thinking, and allows for greater precision and wider use of the researcher's voice in the reporting of the study. In conjunction with the process benefits I discussed earlier, these product benefits are further evidence of the contributions that a research journal can make to the research process.

Conclusion

I have aimed to highlight the potential that keeping a research journal has for enhancing the writer's understanding of the research process. The technique itself is a flexible one, allowing for a range of formats and procedures, and in writing a journal it is important to find those which best suit your own style. Following some basic advice such as writing regularly and engaging with yourself spontaneously and openly is central to the effectiveness of the process. Engaging in the range of reflective processes that journal writing allows can also lead to the kinds of benefits I have outlined here. The narrative I started this chapter with illustrates clearly how the journal can provide crucial support to you at times of difficulty in your research. But the journal is far more than a therapeutic tool and can lend concrete support to you in developing your understanding of the research process.

In conclusion, apart from benefiting the writer, journals may be of value to other readers. Just as teachers' stories of their experience give insight into what being a teacher means, which is instructive for other teachers (Thomas, 1995), so too can the research journal give insight into what doing research in TESOL and what being a TESOL researcher involves. Walford (1991) argues that research textbooks often provide idealized models of research bereft of the complexities, ambiguities, unanticipated difficulties, personal struggles, and conflicts that doing research involves. When novice researchers encounter such undocumented aspects of the research process, they "tend to see these as personal deficiencies arising from insufficient preparation, knowledge, or experience" (p. 2). Thus the insight into the personal side of research that journals can provide is an important addition to existing forms of knowledge about TESOL research that can lend particular support to novices in the field. The full text of my journal would, I believe, give ample support for these arguments, and even the one extract I have provided here begins to shed light on diverse aspects of researchers' experience. Particularly in the education of researchers, even short extracts can serve as the basis of fruitful analysis and discussion of issues in research, something I have done with graduate students.

Resources

Bailey, K. M. (1990). The use of diary studies in teacher education programs. In D. Nunan (Ed.), *Second language teacher education* (pp. 215–226). Cambridge: Cambridge University Press.

Borg, S. (2001). The research journal: A tool for promoting and understanding researcher development. *Language Teaching Research, 5,* 156–177.

In this article I present further extracts from my research journal and discuss in more detail the processes they illustrate and their benefits.

Francis, D. (1995). The reflective journal: A window to preservice teachers' practical knowledge. *Teaching and Teacher Education, 11,* 229–241.

Holly, M. L. (1989a). Reflective writing and the spirit of inquiry. *Cambridge Journal of Education, 19,* 71–80.

Holly, M. L. (1989b). *Writing to grow: Keeping a personal-professional journal.* Portsmouth, NH: Heinemann.

This is a book-length discussion of the role of keeping a journal in professional development. Though not specifically about research journals, it contains much insight into and guidance on the process of keeping a reflective journal in an educational context.

Hoover, L. A. (1994). Reflective writing as a window on preservice teachers' thought processes. *Teaching & Teacher Education, 10,* 83–93.

Janesick, V. J. (1999). A journal about journal writing as a qualitative research technique: History, issues, reflections. *Qualitative Inquiry, 5,* 505–524.

The author uses examples from her own research journal to discuss the processes and the benefits of journal writing for researchers doing qualitative work. She also gives an overview of the historical background to journal writing.

Lamb, A., & Johnson, L. (1999). *Journal writing.* Retrieved February 22, 2002, from http://eduscapes.com/42explore/journl.htm

This site includes links to several sites on journal writing that provide much advice on starting and keeping a journal.

Numrich, C. (1996). On becoming a language teacher: Insights from diary studies. *TESOL Quarterly, 30,* 131–153.

Thomas, D. (1995). Treasonable or trustworthy text. In D. Thomas (Ed.), *Teachers' stories* (pp. 1–23). Buckingham, England: Open University Press.

Thomas discusses the importance of narrative and story (of which journals are an example) in promoting and understanding professional development. The book from which this chapter is taken contains readable accounts of different kinds of teachers' stories.

Walford, G. (1991). Reflexive accounts of doing educational research. In G. Walford (Ed.), *Doing educational research* (pp. 1–18). London: Routledge.

Contributor

Simon Borg (s.borg@education.leeds.ac.uk; http://education.leeds .ac.uk/devt/research/sborg.htm) is senior lecturer in TESOL at the School of Education, University of Leeds, in the United Kingdom. His key areas of interest are language teacher cognition, grammar teaching, and practitioner research. He is also joint coordinator for the International Association of Teachers of English as a Foreign Language's Research Special Interest Group.

6 How Would PhD Feel After Your Name?

Patricia L. Miller

Narrative

At 59 I am running a marathon—not of miles but of words, thoughts, and concepts. Tuesday through Thursday I teach, but from Friday, when the real marathon begins, until Monday, I toil through books and journals, do online research, and carry bags of books to and from the University of Maryland, which grants me library privileges while I finish my doctoral work in composition and TESOL at Indiana University of Pennsylvania (IUP).

When I defended my research proposal in the domain of second language acquisition (SLA) in the summer of 2002, I had been working on the dissertation proposal itself for almost a year. Before that I had spent 6 months preparing for comprehensive examinations in SLA, teacher education, and literacy. Preceding the examinations were 2 years of course work at IUP. With the acceptance of my proposal, at this writing I am beginning a year of research on how successful, advanced ESL academic writers maximize *affordances* (Gibson's, 1986, ecological term that views learning as interaction between the learner and the environment) to master discourse and grammatical competency, followed by another period of time for the writing of the dissertation. I expect to graduate in either 2003 or 2004, when I am 60 or 61. A 6- or 7-year marathon is a long one; the road, however, has been paved with such thick layers of knowledge and deep self-awareness, and such opportunities for lifelong learning, that I have never looked back.

Pursuing a PhD in TESOL and composition is something to dream and talk about doing, but the idea is ephemeral and sly, taking shape and then vanishing, only to appear again. What motivates an individual with already a full career in the field of TESOL to reach deep into her pockets and basically put her life on hold for 7 years? For me, a principal reason was professional development. Although activities such as attending conventions, reading journals, and writing articles had already enriched my expertise, the more I learned, the more I wanted to know. I was, as one professor described me, "hungry for knowledge."

However, the desire to deepen my knowledge was not incentive enough for me to take action. I think a midcareer decision to pursue doctoral work actually has to do with fundamental questions of personal happiness: What do we want to do in our lives, and do we have the credentials to do it? Fortunately, I was shocked into awareness by life's circumstances. The government contract under which I was teaching was not renewed, and I found myself applying for jobs I thought I had the experience for but not getting hired: "I'm sorry, you are qualified, but we are really looking for someone with a PhD." As I saw employment doors close, I began to envision the direction of my life for the next 20 years. At that crossroads I decided to follow my passion for learning—the pursuit of a PhD. Returning to doctoral studies after years in the profession was not easy; however, it has been a rewarding experience of ongoing growth and renewal through a wonderful smorgasbord of professional development opportunities. In this chapter I describe two new roles resulting from reflection on my doctoral course work and illustrate how I grounded theory in practice. I then explain a range of professional development opportunities available to the PhD student and explore a series of considerations from making the initial decision for PhD study to preparing for that new culture.

Role 1: Expert and Participant Observer

I was sitting in TESOL Methodology 721, a required course, surrounded by new students once again. This time, however, I was seated among them, or at least I was trying to be one of them, listening to my professor explain the course syllabus. I heard the professor's words, "This course merges two traditional components of teacher education: teacher preparation for the novice teacher and education for the experienced teacher, or teacher development" (Wallace, 1991). As I looked at all the young faces around the room, I suspected there were many novices; I wondered about their experience and, further, wondered whether I would be the oldest student at 55. Through the introductions, I discovered an interesting mix of native countries and EFL and ESL experience ranging from 1 to 10 years. When it was my turn, I said proudly, "I have 25 years' experience." Heads turned, eyes widened, and the professor smiled. "Hmm, you have more experience than I do." So there I was, clearly in graduate school to learn but already set up as "the expert."

Initially, being a so-called expert was challenging because I soon realized that I needed to modify my tendency to immediately contribute to discussions. As students, we all needed the chance to work through our ideas before being influenced by the expert. This modification sharpened my listening skills, and I became a participant observer, watching our professor make decisions and explore his teaching (Gebhard & Oprandy, 1999). We students also became explorers of our beliefs and practices, seeking awareness so that we could make informed decisions about our teaching. For instance, we learned how to describe our teaching, view it nonjudgmentally, and then explore it by making small changes (Fanselow, 1977, 1988; Gebhard, 1996; Gebhard & Oprandy, 1999). In so doing we came to agree with Edge and Richards (1998), who posit that there is no single best way to teach.

I grounded my practice in theory: By listening, observing, and exploring our teaching, I saw others, as well as I, gain understanding of what we do and why we do it. This awareness produced confidence in my teaching decisions, and I found I had achieved some measure of autonomy and become an empowered teacher. Today, I make many more decisions than I did in the past; however, with autonomy comes responsibility—there is an institution that must be respected. The difference now is that I have not only the desire but also the courage to contribute my opinions regarding effective practice.

Role 2: Developing My Own Voice and Hearing the Other Voices

Inherent in doctoral education is the development of academic beliefs. I believe the ability to take positions on the academic and human questions that confront the TESOL profession demands a strong spoken and written voice. Elbow's idea of voice (as cited in Harris, 1996) is that it resonates each person's uniqueness. Harris extends this idea to include selfhood, with implications of "breath, spirit, and presence" (p. 24). In retrospect, many of my professors subtly encouraged the development of our unique voices, validating our selfhood by accepting our comments and finding some thread of meaning to build on our arguments. Our classes were not necessarily communities building a consensus on a single right interpretation of a text, for instance, but were instead, in the words of Pratt (1998), a *contact zone*, where conflicting views and discourses met and where what we said or wrote was respected as heterogeneous voices, ones that could not be directed.

I grounded practice in theory: The notions of voice and the contact zone have shaped my practice. Different perspectives and perceptions are welcome in my classes. Furthermore, I try to not respond negatively to students' comments, looking for a grain of truth to expand. Even with comments that seem appropriate, I try to avoid excessive evaluative responses and instead encourage additional perspective. The result, according to my students, is that they feel empowered—they have a voice.

Steps _____

Making the Journey From Decision to University

1. Give careful consideration to choosing a university. The process from initial search to university acceptance took about 8 months. To begin, I reviewed the PhD programs listed in

TESOL's *Directory of Professional Preparation Programs in TESOL in the United States and Canada, 1999–2001* (Garshick, 1998). I was looking for a practical program in which I could utilize my TESOL experience, that emphasized qualitative research, that was intensive so that I could complete my course work as soon as possible, and that was within my financial means. TESOL's directory enabled me to focus my search. Telephone conversations with program directors and several campus visits followed the program review. I finally settled on IUP's PhD in TESOL and composition, two areas of study I wanted to pursue. Located in the small and peaceful town of Indiana, the campus was only a 4-hour drive from my house.

2. Find an appropriate living environment. After a December acceptance, I had just a month to find accommodations. I had to give serious thought to my living arrangements because any anxiety regarding my accommodations would affect my studies. Although the university recommended its efficiency dormitory apartments, I had already been on campus and seen the high level of activity of dorm life. I had also investigated requests for roommates through the Housing Office, but every telephone inquiry was accompanied by music that could shatter the quiet essential for my intensive study. Finally, I settled on a semifurnished apartment near the university so I could walk to class. I frequented yard sales to furnish the apartment and never did buy a bed, sleeping instead on a futon on the floor, advantageous on hot summer nights without air-conditioning. I was a student again. On some weekends I commuted home, and on others, my husband and dogs commuted to Indiana.

3. Get to know your new culture. During the university selection process, I had visited potential campuses and met with program coordinators, students (a good source of information), and some professors. For IUP in particular, I had a thorough understanding of the program's offerings and the direction my studies might take, and I had done some research on the professors who generally taught my courses, including their publications. Because I would be spending considerable time with some of them, I wanted to ensure that our interests would

coincide. Unfortunately, I did not arrive on the IUP campus in time for an orientation; as a result, I was on my own locating everything from dining halls to health facilities. With time being the quintessential precious commodity for a PhD student, I could ill afford a leisurely exploration of campus; it was a long time before I knew key sites. Consequently, I recommend learning locations and procedures before the semester begins.

Sampling the Smorgasbord of Professional Development Opportunities

Although many professional development opportunities are available to doctoral students, I chose to pursue three:

1. Seek out possibilities for collaboration with faculty on presentations, publications, and research.

   - Another student and I were invited by our SLA professor to collaborate on a panel entitled "Focus on Form—Preventing Errors" and present our individual research at the 1999 Pennsylvania University Teachers Convention in Millersville, Pennsylvania. Several meetings enabled us not only to extend our ideas through our professor's scaffolding but also to contribute to his ideas. Working this closely with faculty gives valuable mentoring experience.

   - One of the assignments in a class on second language literacy was to review a literacy book for the class. After doing the assignment, I thought I knew the book well enough to review it for publication but felt I lacked the background knowledge to situate it in the field. The professor agreed to collaborate, and our review of Zamel and Spack's *Negotiating Academic Literacies* (1998) was published in the Teacher Education Interest Section *TEIS Newsletter* (Tannacito & Miller, 1999).

2. Apply for research grants, including student/faculty research grants. Most universities award several grants competitively to PhD students. The one I applied for was a student/faculty research grant under the University Senate Research Committee, which holds seven competitions throughout the year for grants

to a maximum of $1,500. The focus can be on either the graduate student's research or that of a faculty member. I was the recipient of a student/faculty grant in 1999 to work with my SLA professor on "A Survey on the Oral Proficiency of Non-Native English Speakers in U.S. M.A. TESOL Programs." This grant not only provided opportunity for further guidance but also opened doors to the University's Research Center and its benefits.

3. Investigate special award possibilities. Many opportunities are available for graduate assistantships, either with professors or in other aspects of the program, and teaching assistantships at the university's English language program or in undergraduate classes. Moreover, you may be able to uncover a need that fits your experience. As a result of my experience with testing, including oral proficiency testing, I received a special appointment as the director of testing at the American Language Institute on campus.

Conclusion

My life has not really been on hold as I study for my PhD; doctoral study is my life. What *on hold* means to me is that I cannot yet have the job I am studying for. What will eventually be a 7-year period of study has been a roller coaster of emotions accompanying intensive learning and development, each phase deeper than the preceding one, until I have recognized that I really do possess a knowledge base, not only under and supporting me but surrounding me and touching my students. Now I am beginning to feel the meaning of the initials *PhD* I hope to have after my name.

Resources

Edge, J., & Richards, K. (1998). Why best practice is not good enough. *TESOL Quarterly, 32,* 569–575.

Fanselow, J. F. (1977). Beyond "Rashomon"—conceptualizing and describing the teaching act. *TESOL Quarterly, 11,* 17–39.

Fanselow, J. F. (1988). "Let's see": Contrasting conversations about teaching. *TESOL Quarterly, 22,* 113–130.

Garshick, E. (Ed.). (1998). *Directory of professional preparation programs in TESOL in the United States and Canada, 1999–2001.* Alexandria, VA: TESOL.

Garshick, E. (Ed.). (2002). *Directory of teacher education programs in TESOL in the United States and Canada, 2002–2004.* Alexandria, VA: TESOL.

The 2002–2004 directory lists 28 doctoral programs in TESOL, providing information on the particular degree, program length and requirements, course offerings, administration requirements, cost, background information, full-time faculty, and contact information.

Gebhard, J. (1996). *Teaching English as a foreign language: A self-development and methodology guide.* Ann Arbor: University of Michigan Press.

Gebhard, J., & Oprandy, R. (1999). *Language teaching awareness: A guide to exploring beliefs and practices.* New York: Cambridge University Press.

Gibson, J. J. (1986). *The ecological approach to visual perception.* Hillsdale, NJ: Erlbaum.

Harris, J. (1996). *A teaching subject: Composition since 1996.* Upper Saddle River, NJ: Prentice Hall.

Pratt, M. L. (1998). Arts of the contact zone. In V. Zamel & R. Spack (Eds.), *Negotiating academic literacies: Teaching and learning across languages and cultures* (pp. 171–186). Mahwah, NJ: Erlbaum.

Tannacito, D. J., & Miller, P. L. (1999, September). BookBlurb: Zamel, V. & Spack, R. (1998). *Negotiating academic literacies: Teaching and learning across languages and cultures. Teacher Education Interest Section Newsletter, 15,* 8, 11.

van Lier, L. (2000). From input to affordance: Social-interactive learning from an ecological perspective. In J. P. Lantolf (Ed.), *Sociocultural theory and second language learning* (pp. 245–259). New York: Oxford University Press.

Wallace, M. (1991). *Training foreign language teachers.* New York: Cambridge University Press.

Zamel, V., & Spack, R. (Eds.). (1998). *Negotiating academic literacies: Teaching and learning across languages and cultures.* Mahwah, NJ: Erlbaum.

Contributor

Patricia L. Miller (patricialmiller@starpower.net), an associate professor of English, teaches academic writing at Montgomery College, Maryland, in the United States. She has spent many years working in the TESOL profession in and outside the United States. At this writing she expects to receive her doctorate in composition and TESOL in spring 2004.

7 | Net Gains

Catherine Green

Narrative _____

It was somewhat by chance that I found myself sitting in on one of the very last presentations scheduled for the final day of the 32nd Annual TESOL Convention in Seattle, Washington, in 1998. Pregnant, tired, but excited by the preceding 4 packed days, I was scheduled to go to the airport to return to my hectic life at home and work. For months I had dreamed that I would find some way to rearrange my life so that I could choose where I wanted to live, have a flexible work schedule, work from home, and, best of all, have more opportunities for educating ESOL teachers, especially those from other countries. If only I could telecommute, I thought, but it seemed impossible.

At least it did until that day at TESOL, when I listened to a pair of presenters talking about online teaching. By the end of the talk, they had convinced me that such a life was indeed possible. Not only that, the presenters allayed one of my greatest fears and showed me how online teachers could create a sense of community, developing a rapport with a group of far-flung learners they could neither see nor hear.

Two months later, I was enrolled in an online seminar about teaching via the Internet, and that fall I taught my first online course, Teaching Writing. Since then, I have been able to work from home, care for my two young children, live in a lovely community in the foothills of the Sierra Nevada mountains, and be stimulated every day by my challenging work with teachers and teachers-to-be scattered around the United States and the world. Our exchanges are often lively, our comments remarkably reflective, and our perspectives broadened by each individual's own experiences as a learner and teacher. This is especially true when we are fortunate enough to have participants logging in from different corners of the world, many of whom could not have otherwise found similar opportunities for professional development in their immediate locations. In writing this article, I realize just how lucky I am to have found work with such a great fit.

Before trying online teaching, I had my share of doubts about it, of course. Would I like working by myself, sitting at my computer, rather than moving around a noisy room full of smiling faces? How could I ensure that everyone would participate fully? Could I find enough job opportunities to make this lifestyle really work? Could I be efficient enough to provide quality input, reflection, and feedback while not spending so much time online that I was reducing my pay rate to mere pennies per hour? Finally, was I Internet and techno-savvy enough to handle all of this?

The answer to all these questions has been a resounding *yes*. Though not without its pitfalls, teaching online has helped me develop in a number of ways. In this chapter I discuss how to create a successful online course, how to avoid some of the pitfalls, and what the potential net gains are.

Description

Online TESOL education work varies a great deal in format and nature, though all forms rely heavily on the written word. One type is set up along the lines of regular on-site classes, in which a group of learners work to complete a course within a set time frame (e.g., a quarter or semester). The size of the group may vary from 5 to more than 40, with the most common ratios being 8–25 learners per teacher. Participants often work asynchronously, logging on at different times to accomplish their weekly goals. Another type of course operates in real time, but if the teacher is located in Australia, for example, some of the participants on other continents may find they must get up at 3:00 a.m. to go to class.

In addition, some of these courses utilize software programs (e.g., Blackboard Learning System, 2002; WebCT, 2002) or Web-based classroom systems (e.g., NiceNet's Internet Classroom Assistant, http://www.nicenet.org) that operate much like a bulletin board, with participants posting separate messages and replying to each other's postings, while other programs channel the discussions into single threads or subconferences through which participants scroll. Additional basic tools include e-mail and chat rooms. All the systems offer at least some technical support (ideally available around the clock), thereby leaving the instructor and participants free to concentrate on the academic content and discussions, not the technology.

Along with composing messages and reading and responding to others' postings, learners in some programs may be able to take advantage of other forms of communication with each other or the instructor. For example, participants may speak with their instructor by telephone in established office hours or, in other cases, use a video camera and speakers to see and hear their instructor, much like distance learning via satellite broadcast.

Steps

There is no set way to create or teach courses online, though many universities that offer them also provide training to faculty. The following are the steps that I took in preparing and teaching my online courses, and you can certainly adjust your approach based on your needs and situation. The Resources section below offers additional references on finding, evaluating, and sampling online courses and programs.

Preparing the Course

1. Scope out university Web sites. Frequently, universities with online programs will allocate some of their Web site to a description of the program, highlighting such information as technical requirements, types of environments, types of classes offered, enrollment figures (by class and by program), contact points for further information, and requirements for participants. For help in finding and evaluating university online programs, see the Resources section, particularly the Distance Learning Resource Network's Web site.

2. Learn about the process and content of online courses. Most likely you will receive some software training from your institution. Take this opportunity to (a) learn the content and, perhaps more important, (b) learn about the process of facilitating and organizing an online course. In general, be aware that, in teaching teachers, you will in effect be modeling a way for them to approach their own courses and learners. Thus, using friendly greetings, actively facilitating discussions, and providing a structured syllabus and a clear set of expectations are all strategies that would serve your participants and their learners well, whether online or on-site.

3. Create a wide variety of tasks and assignments that will appeal to different types of learners. A number of the types of tasks I use are experiential and reflective in nature. For example, in my course on teaching writing, participants read a student's piece of writing, then give feedback to the learner as if they were his or her teachers. Afterward, participants read each others' feedback to the same student, analyzing the pros and cons of each and reflecting on how they can apply what they have learned from this experience to their situation. Other collaborative task types include debates, case studies, simulations, and role plays (for a discussion, see Ko & Rossen, 2001).

   Another very popular and appropriate assignment for online TESOL courses is a research paper on Web resources: In my classes, participants scout out at least 10–20 sites and report on a handful of them, noting their strengths and weaknesses for teaching English language learners. Afterward, participants read everyone else's research to discover new sites relevant to their context. In addition to completing assignments such as these, I require participants to respond to at least three colleagues' comments each week, thus fostering more interaction among learners.

For input, utilize as broad a range as possible, including lectures (i.e., an article written by the teacher, sometimes with links to relevant Web sites embedded in it), small and large peer-group discussions, published textbooks, articles and other information on Web sites, guest speakers, classroom observations, CD-ROMs, video excerpts, and other media.

4. Explore a range of ways to evaluate and give feedback on your participants' process and products. I have used objective tests and essay exams as well as electronic portfolios to assess what and how the participants are learning. Journals are another important feature of my courses and are especially well suited to online learning. In my classes, participants keep a weekly journal, which is written primarily for their eyes only. Participants may select excerpts to share with their small discussion group, but later on, in their portfolios, participants include direct quotes from their journal as they trace and expand on a recurring theme. In sharing their comments with others online, whether in response to an assignment or to another colleague's remark, participants realize the potential of online learning to promote reflection and thoughtful writing: Many people work harder at organizing their thoughts when putting them down in writing, and if a contribution is published and read on the World Wide Web, participants tend to write even more carefully.

Teaching the Course

5. Welcome each participant with a virtual handshake. In my experience, this component is a key for successful online learning experiences. It is well worth it to personally greet participants individually soon after they have bravely come

online and introduced themselves. Working in isolation, participants may feel especially anxious and need extra support. Be encouraging and warm, and use all your icebreaking skills to put them at ease: Chat with them, using their names to speak to them directly, and draw them out with friendly questions about their personal as well as their professional lives. Post a picture of yourself, and encourage participants to do the same.

6. Pave the way for your participants during the first week or two.

- Devote the first week to all kinds of introductions, and aim to make any required reading available online (either an article you have posted or a link to a Web site with relevant readings), because some learners, especially those working in remote locations, may have difficulty getting their textbooks before Day 1 of class. I tend to spend at least twice as much time as in later weeks ensuring that by the end of Week 1 all participants are clear about my expectations and their role and feel encouraged to try out this new medium of instruction.

- Break up a large class (i.e., one with more than 10 participants) into small groups, and give participants a social task (e.g., go on a scavenger hunt, find someone according to certain criteria, or just chat to discover what they have in common) that will encourage them to bond with at least a small group of participants. If you can, follow up with a quick e-mail to individual participants in Week 1 or 2 to see how they are feeling about the course.

- Very early on in the course, remind online learners about the power of the written word and the need for tolerance, encouraging them to give everyone the benefit of the doubt when misunderstandings occur. It is easy for misinterpretations to happen in an online class, as immediate clarification is not possible, and there are no nonverbal cues. Once in print (especially in capital letters on the World Wide Web), words take on larger significance than they might in a spontaneous discussion in an on-site class.

7. Facilitate discussion and encourage full participation during the course. Throughout the course online learners may need continuing guidance and encouragement from you, especially because they cannot hear or see anyone in this new learning environment. In online learning, repetition is considered beneficial, as some learners have trouble remembering where to find certain information in their virtual classroom. To help my learners track what is due when, I post a schedule of assignments in a central place, then each week present an overview that recaps the assignments due that week.

   In addition, each week's plenary forum includes a discussion thread for asking questions about assignments. As the instructor, I also check attendance regularly (via a tracking system embedded in the software programs I use), notice how often learners have posted comments, and evaluate how in-depth or superficial their reflections are. When they fall behind, I e-mail the individuals right away and offer support, while reminding them of my expectations for their participation; indeed, when the class exists only in cyberspace, there is less loss of face in not showing up for class, and, consequently, a few participants may need an extra e-mail reminder from the instructor.

8. Get feedback from your learners on the quality of their online learning experience. If you have never taught online before, this step is critical. I usually survey a number of issues in an end-of-term questionnaire and elicit participants' feedback throughout the course. You can also ask for feedback from the contacts you have made at the faculty online training seminar.

Conclusion

My journey into teaching in the virtual classroom has not been without its bumps or unexpected detours. I do, on occasion, miss the immediacy and spontaneity of on-site exchanges, and when teaching a lot of online classes at once, I have to work harder at keeping track of who is who in this asynchronous and faceless environment. I now have to reach well beyond my work environment to help satisfy my social needs, and I must also force myself to move around more physically. I have certainly become more techno-savvy than I was when I started this work, though I am grateful that the technical learning curve, for me, at least, was not as steep as I had feared. As a freelance consultant in a new medium of instruction, I have to keep looking out for myself to ensure that I will find enough work online. Additionally, sometimes I struggle to keep the number of hours I am online in keeping with the number of contact hours of the on-site course counterpart; when I exceed that number, the glowing feedback I receive from participants helps offset the monetary losses.

Despite—or perhaps partly because of—these bumps and detours, I have grown a lot, personally and professionally. Making frequent and nearly instantaneous connections with participants around the globe has been exhilarating, especially when I can see that the work we do together can make a difference in their lives and, more important, in their learners' lives. I also experience vicarious pleasure in being able to imagine myself teaching in these foreign contexts, and it puts my skills as an EFL teacher and teacher educator to the test daily. Watching how participants expand their world views, as they begin to reexamine their role as teachers of English language learners in a global context and expand their sense of professional community, has been gratifying, too. In addition, I have loved using a medium of instruction that seems to lend itself so naturally to promoting reflection. Last but not least, I am glad that I have been able to make such a major change in lifestyle, making my dream—being there for my family, helping spare the Earth by not commuting, and having thought-provoking and satisfying work—come true. In conclusion, though you certainly need to invest something of yourself—your time, your energy, and maybe a faster Internet connection—in order to teach online, the net gains are well worth it.

Resources

Blackboard Learning System [Computer software]. (2002). Washington, DC: Blackboard. Available from http:// www.blackboard.com

Distance Learning Resource Network. http://www.dlrn.org

> This site provides a number of useful tips, including criteria for selecting, designing, and evaluating an online course. There are also links to several sample online courses in a variety of subjects.

Ko, S., & Rossen, S. (2001). *Teaching online: A practical guide.* New York: Houghton Mifflin.

> This very complete and practical resource for first-timers also offers new insights and suggestions for seasoned online teachers.

TESOL. http://www.tesol.org

> For additional resources related to this chapter, go to the Publications section of the site and click on the link to this book in "Browse the Catalog."

WebCT [Computer software]. (2002). Lynnfield, MA: WebCT. Available from http://www.webct.com

Contributor

Catherine Green (catherine_green@mindspring.com) is a teacher educator working online with two universities, University of California, Los Angeles, and The New School for Social Research, New York, in the United States, and is coauthor of the two-volume *Tasks for Teacher Education: A Reflective Approach* (Pearson Education, 1998). Her professional interests include distance learning via the Internet, reflective teaching, and educating EFL teachers internationally.

8 Growing With the Flow: Sustaining Professionalism Through Online Instruction of Language Teachers

Faridah Pawan and Anna Jacobson

Narrative _____

Faridah

Twice in my teaching career I have faced classes in which a former teacher was one of my students. The first time, I was a recent college graduate teaching a traditional ESL methods class in Malaysia. On the second occasion, I was teaching my first online class. Would they think that I measured up as a mentor, I wondered?

In both instances, I faced the challenge of finding ways to balance my role as an instructor with my need to learn the subject matter. In the case of online classes, I also had to learn the idiosyncrasies of a new medium for teaching. As an instructor, I wanted to assure my students (and my former mentors) that I could provide leadership. At the same time, I wanted to create opportunities for myself to participate as a colearner so that I could bring my own expertise up to speed.

Anna

In my first experience as a teacher educator, one of my former high school students asked me to be her cooperating teacher. I had only been teaching myself for 4 years and was not sure I would be up to the challenge. It turned out to be a terrific mentoring opportunity. My student teacher and I learned together, and we became close friends as well as colleagues.

The first time I did teacher education online, I had left my high school teaching job and was in my first semester of doctoral work. I became an online teacher on the advice of a professor mainly because I was curious about how online courses worked. I was pleasantly surprised; my online class consisted of practicing ESL/EFL teachers. They were people I could relate to as fellow teachers, and I felt I could share what I was learning with them as well as be their guide in the new world of online education.

Description

Becoming a teacher educator is the next level of the profession that many language teachers move to after many years of classroom teaching. When we made this move, we realized that we would outgrow some of our mentors and be perceived as mentors in our own right. We had to convince our teacher learners that we knew what we were doing while learning to be professionally accountable online teacher educators. For us, this transformation meant using *telementoring* (Wighton, 1993) skills to build an online community, enhancing online interactions through collaborative learning, and adopting constructivist approaches to increase the authenticity of experience.

Steps

Using Telementoring Skills to Build a Community Online

Building a community online was very important to us for several reasons. We were aware that the absence of teacher-student interaction has been reported as one of the factors leading to increased dropout rates among distant learners. We knew we had to adapt our mentoring skills for use in telecommunication media, such as e-mail and electronic discussion lists. In our case, we sought a symbiotic mentoring relationship; we support our students through interactive, online discourse, and they support us with invaluable insights into our online teaching.

1. Establish a human presence. When we first started to teach online, most of our students were taking Web-based classes for the first time and were not used to the physical absence of instructors and classmates. To alleviate the discomfort caused by this absence, we incorporated four different ways to interact through a combination of synchronous and asynchronous applications. We use Tapped In (a synchronous, multiuser Web-based application; http://www.tappedin.sri.com/) and SiteScape Forum (2002; asynchronous group collaboration software) for formal discussions and meetings, and MSN Instant Messenger (synchronous) and e-mail (asynchronous) for a mixture of informal and formal discussions and chats.

   These multiple ways for participants to connect with one another provide avenues for the frequent and open sharing of thoughts, ideas, and insecurities. Besides being critical in creating a bond among members of the class, the electronic means of discourse allows us, as novice online instructors, to be more open about our challenges in online teaching. We often receive "reverse mentoring" and counseling from our students. For example, in one class, when we experienced difficulty in convincing students to use Tapped In, one of our students suggested that we share the reasons and ways we used Tapped In with our own work. The student reminded us that we needed to give the class a model of the practical value of the application from our own teaching experience. In addition, the student suggested that we make transparent the preparation involved in organizing synchronous discussions on Tapped In so that everyone could see how to use it in their own online courses. The non-face-to-face nature of interacting through the tools mentioned above allows students to be direct with us. The results can be gratifying as well as painful, but they are always useful.

2. Establish a buddy system. After the first 2 weeks of class, when students have become acquainted with one another, we ask them to select one or two class members to be their buddies, the people to whom they first go for questions and comments. We also link current students to former students, which helps us sort out logistical and technical difficulties.

3. Be proactive. Some of our telementoring falls within the domain of the *virtual handshake* (see chapter 7). For example, as soon as students register online, we have them upload their photographs to the discussion forum and establish "help" folders in which students post questions and receive answers. We also create locations ahead of time in our forum to which students upload drafts of homework so that everyone can see what is expected of them and gauge their own progress. (Grades, of course, are sent to students privately.) Students are encouraged (and at times assigned) to ask questions and make suggestions on each other's work. The bonus for us is that the students help us see issues that may otherwise have gone unnoticed. An example is the issue of access: We have learned that not all students can access Web sites and online resources that we suggest because of institutional and national censorship policies on Internet use. As a result, we now give alternatives to research-based assignments using the Internet.

Enhancing Online Interactions Through Collaboration

Our early struggles with teaching in a computer-mediated environment involved several challenges in mediating interactions. We continually work to increase collaboration in ways that benefit our students and our instruction.

1. Assign roles if participation is inconsistent. Similar to classroom discussions, some students dominate online discussions while others merely read the discussions without participating. To address this, each week we designate different students as *starters, provocateurs,* and *wrappers.* Starters are responsible for raising issues from the weekly readings, asking questions, and encouraging class members to make connections between the readings and their experiences. Most

important, the starters must try to keep everybody on track in discussions. The provocateurs' role is to provide a contrary perspective and challenge opinions. Finally, the task of the wrappers is to summarize discussion themes at the end of each weekly session and suggest readings for future reference and discussion. In assuming those roles, students must participate more regularly; in addition, instructors are freed up to give individual attention to students needing help.

2. Encourage collaborative discourse. In online discourse, serial monologues tend to predominate over collaborative discourse characterized by challenge-and-explain cycles of interaction (Curtis & Lawson, 1999). Essentially, students tend to be more focused on writing about their own thoughts than on connecting with those of their classmates. As a consequence, they tend to write very long monologues in response to prompts and do not come together as a community. To overcome this challenge, we have students take a metacognitive approach. We and the students monitor participation through postings on the forum by labeling them (e.g., *initiate, question, express agreement/disagreement, confirm, elaborate, summarize, request information*). We also ask students to limit their postings to 100–150 words (without limiting the frequency of postings) so that students do not have to read a voluminous amount of textual information online or lose track of what they read in lengthy postings. Also, we ask students to develop *hooks*— provocative questions, issues, or points whose main purpose is to stir up a reaction from classmates—at the end of each of their postings.

Through these modifications, our students have made more attempts to react to each other's thoughts, and for the most part they have been willing to follow the trains of thought that others suggest. In return, we have learned to monitor our input.

Increasing Authenticity of Experience

We define *authenticity of experience* as the utilization and validation of our students' personal knowledge in class discussions and projects, even though teachers often think that their day-to-day teaching is routine (Ellsworth, 1989; Yonemura, 1986). Authenticity of experience allows students to share and reflect on the realities of their professional lives and to engage in those of others.

We take a constructivist instructional approach to reach our authenticity objectives. Abdal-Haqq (1998), citing works by Canella and Reiff (1994) and Richardson (1997), maintains that in constructivism "individuals create or construct their own new understandings or knowledge through the interaction of what they already know and believe and the ideas, events, and activities with which they come in contact" (para. 1). To create an environment in which this is possible, we first worked on developing a solid, instructor-generated structure, which is a prerequisite for the effective functioning of online classes (Warschauer & Meskill, 2000). Through the asynchronous online discussion forum, this structure becomes student centered. For example, because the forum is asynchronous, responses from the instructors and the students can appear any time during the week; we, the instructors, do not always have the first word or the final say, allowing students to shape the objectives of the classes. Because of this, students with different professional and personal experiences often bring an interdisciplinary approach to a topic, linking language teaching with, for instance, content in history or science along with the corresponding online resources. We benefit as instructors because we can learn about these content-based connections to language teaching and learning.

Below we describe the initial course structure and explain how we make provisions for change.

1. Begin with problem-based contexts. We start each class with problem contexts or incidences that lead into theoretical analyses and discussions. An ESL child's fear of test taking, for example, starts a discussion on alternative assessment. We then turn our attention to students' problems in their classrooms or teaching situations. Using our readings and experiences, we work together to understand the problems, and come up with options and, at times, even a solution or two. The frequent presence of content area teachers often inspires language teachers in our online language education classes to contemplate cross-disciplinary solutions. In addition, because

our enrollments cross national boundaries, the problems we discuss are cross-cultural. We echo Green's sentiment (see chapter 7) that teaching online is enlightening and exhilarating, allowing us to interact and discuss issues with practicing teachers from around the globe.

2. Assign reflective papers. Our students engage in a continuous process of self-observation and self-assessment. Every 2 weeks, the students write reflective papers that evaluate their beliefs, practices, and learning in light of our class readings, discussions, and projects. Through these reflections, students have opportunities to take conscious control of their own learning and contextualize the class within their own circumstances with an eye to refining their practice. Information from the reflections often then becomes part of the problem contexts that drive our discussions. Through these reflections, we learn what issues are important to students. More important, every so often we see our teaching having an impact in our students' teaching practice. This is important for sustaining confidence in ourselves as effective instructors who are professionally in touch with our students even though we are physically distant from them.

3. Set up resource-sharing folders. The classroom discussion forum for our class includes folders through which students share resources, ask for help with difficult situations, and share teacherly wisdom. The resources contribute greatly to our collection of up-to-date, available materials.

Conclusion

Teaching online classes has given us the means to rediscover our teaching. It has allowed us to take a new look at and reassess what we know about good teaching. The new medium and the technology available have enabled us to structure our classes so that we grow professionally with our students' help. In a sense, they have made it possible for us to alternate roles as mentors and mentored.

Resources

Abdal-Haqq, I. (1998). *Constructivism in teacher education.* Washington, DC: ERIC Clearinghouse on Teaching and Teacher Education. Retrieved January 30, 2002, from http://www.ed.gov/databases /ERIC_Digests/ed426986.html (ERIC Document Reproduction Service No. ED 426986)

This article gives definitions of constructivism as both an educational and a social theory.

Curtis, D., & Lawson, M. (1999, July). *Collaborative online learning: An exploratory case study.* Paper presented at the Higher Education Research and Development Society of Australasia Annual International Conference, Melbourne, Australia.

This article focuses on the interactions between students in an online class, examining their postings for examples of collaborative behavior.

Ellsworth, E. (1989). Why doesn't this feel empowering? Working through the repressive myths of critical pedagogy. *Harvard Educational Review, 59,* 297–324.

This author urges that every teacher be an *emancipated authority,* one who has been given authority by students on the basis of expanded knowledge.

SiteScape Forum [Computer software]. (2002). Wilmington, NC: SiteScape. Available from http://www.sitescape.com

Warschauer, M., & Meskill, C. (2000) Technology and second language learning. In J. Rosenthal (Ed.), *Handbook of undergraduate second language education* (pp. 303–318). Mahwah, NJ: Erlbaum.

This article gives guidelines for teaching second languages online as well as examples of language learning classes, noting that structure is important to all of these classes.

Wighton, D. J. (1993). *Telementoring: An examination of the potential for an educational network.* Retrieved January 30, 2002, from http:// mentor.creighton.edu/htm/telement.htm

This paper describes the mentoring role of teachers in online education.

Yonemura, M. (1986). Reflections on teacher empowerment and teacher education. *Harvard Educational Review, 56,* 473–480.

The author describes a teacher education program that seeks to empower its teachers before they begin teaching.

Contributors

Faridah Pawan (fpawan@indiana.edu) is an assistant professor in the Language Education Department at Indiana University Bloomington, in the United States. Her areas of interest include EFL/ESL teaching pedagogy as well as online teacher education and language teaching. She was the 2001 recipient of the TESOL/Heinle & Heinle Award for Excellence in Teaching.

Anna Jacobson (ajacobso@indiana.edu) is a doctoral candidate in the Language Education Department at Indiana University Bloomington, in the United States. Her interests include computer-assisted language learning, less commonly taught languages, and foreign and second language pedagogy.

9 Get Real! Authentic Assessment in Graduate-Level TESOL Programs

Annis N. Shaver, Juliet E. Hart, and Mary A. Avalos

Narrative

Although it has been 3 years since our date with that king of all evaluations, the comprehensive examination, two of us (Annis and Juliet) can still recall (with residual, trace amounts of agony) the weeks of endless cramming, the countless study sessions, guesswork at possible questions, the long, sleep-deprived nights, the many cups of coffee, the anxiety-ridden weeks anticipating the results, and the "brain dump" after confirmation of a passing score.

In the weeks that followed the comprehensive exam in our master's-level TESOL program, we began to reflect on what we had actually learned and whether we really had had the opportunity to demonstrate any of our newly acquired competencies via this traditional form of exam. Furthermore, we pondered the irony of being assessed in a manner that ultimately could not be considered authentic in a program that stressed the necessity of evaluating students in valid and integrative ways, such as through performance and portfolio types of assessments.

Fast forward 3 years. As doctoral research assistants, we were assigned to teach a curriculum course for students in a TESOL teacher education program. In preparing for our first foray into college-level instruction, we engaged in several ongoing discussions about how we would structure the course, what goals and objectives we had for the students, and how the students could be most validly assessed. We shared our very similar experiences and frustrations as master's-level students preparing for our own final course and comprehensive exams, and decided that we should introduce an authentic, alternative method of assessment in the course we would be teaching. We were in search of some form of evaluation that would allow our teacher learners to demonstrate the best teaching practices for use with linguistically diverse learners while providing materials and instructional plans that they could implement in their own classrooms. In collaborative dialogue, our adviser (Mary) recommended portfolio assessment, specifically electronic portfolios.

Thus, the notion of the paperless portfolio as final evaluation in our master's-level TESOL program was born. Although the three of us had our reservations about our technological expertise (or lack thereof), the amount of work involved, and the students' response to this new evaluative measure, we would learn that the benefits in terms of our growth as professionals and that of the students would far outweigh any of the difficulties we had along the way. Moreover, numerous unanticipated advantages would surface that would serve to solidify this innovative form of assessment as a grounded part of our teacher preparation program.

Description

We set to the task of researching the history of alternative forms of evaluation, including portfolio assessment. A relatively new method of assessment with a history spanning only the past two decades, the usage of portfolios gained momentum as teachers became concerned about the negative effects of testing on their students as well as the lack of validity evident in formal evaluative measures. Although similar to an artist's portfolio, the student portfolio assessment, as defined by McLaughlin and Vogt (1996), is more than a collection of a student's work. It is evidence of (a) a student's comprehension of material taught, (b) interaction between student and teacher(s), (c) a student's progress over time, and (d) a student's reflection on his or her work in the form of self-assessment. An electronic portfolio is an improvement over the paper-based portfolio. It is easy to use, easy to store, easy to search by multiple criteria, and easily updated and copied (Rogers & Williams, 1999). Electronic portfolios have the same contents as paper-based portfolios with the added advantage of direct links to the Internet and from one document to another. Portfolios, therefore, stand in stark contrast to traditional means of assessment, particularly the final comprehensive exam, which in fact gives only a cursory view of the knowledge gained by a student during the course of study and which fails to provide evidence of students' ability to apply what they have learned.

Our goals for establishing an electronic portfolio as the final evaluation for the master's in TESOL dovetailed with the definition of portfolio assessment. Distinguishing features of our electronic assessment included video clips of the students teaching, display of case study materials in electronic form over time, and participation in online discussions of relevant curricular topics. We wanted to provide a means of authentic assessment for the students, the majority of whom were seasoned teachers of all grade levels seeking certification in teaching linguistically diverse learners in multicultural schools. Primarily, we wanted to give these teacher learners the opportunity to exhibit the skills they had acquired and honed during the program while reducing the anxiety associated with a traditional exam.

Steps

Our electronic portfolio assessment was designed in three phases: preparation, implementation, and evaluation. These phases formed a methodological approach that helped us cover all our bases.

Preparing for the Portfolio

1. Review the resources available. There are multiple how-to books describing the design and implementation of portfolio assessment (e.g., Bullock & Hawk, 2001; Campbell, Cignetti,

Melenyzer, Nettles, & Wyman, 1997; McLaughlin & Vogt, 1996; McLaughlin, Vogt, Anderson, DuMez, Peter, & Hunter, 1998; Wilcox & Tomei, 1999). Read as many as possible, and cut and paste from them to design a program that fits your specific needs.

2. Decide on the criteria to be met. Some (electronic) portfolio designs adhere to one set of standards as the basis for the component parts of the assessment. You may, as we did, decide to use multiple standards, including ESL standards (TESOL, 1997), accomplished teaching practices for your state or territory (Florida Education Standards Commission, 1996), or national education board standards (if they exist) for your country (National Board for Professional Teaching Standards, 2001).

3. Choose components of the portfolio that will demonstrate mastery of your objectives and goals. Include optional components in addition to the required ones in order to allow the students an opportunity to demonstrate individual creativity or interests. Some resources provide lists of components that can be used in portfolios. Consider these in addition to designing elements to suit your specific needs. Our portfolio showcased a linguistic assessment case study that integrated multiple standards and course objectives spanning an entire academic year. Students may choose to design an integrated WebQuest (Dodge & March, 1995) as part of the electronic portfolio. A WebQuest is an inquiry-oriented activity in which most or all of the information the learners use is drawn from the Web.

4. Decide on the software to use for your electronic portfolio. We chose Microsoft PowerPoint because it was easily accessible at our university and because many of our teachers were already familiar with it, but many software packages are designed specifically for the production of portfolios. Such programs as Adobe PageMill 3.0 and Microsoft FrontPage 2000 can be used to create Web-based portfolios.

Assigning the Portfolio

5. Provide instruction on software use. We conduct a mandatory workshop for the students on the use of Microsoft PowerPoint (and the use of other forms of technology) for portfolio preparation.

6. Establish portfolio requirements for courses in the program. We familiarize the professors with the requirements and demonstrate how they can include certain components of the portfolio in their course requirements.

7. Monitor progress continually. A portfolio cannot be compiled in a week's time. It is a project that commences at the beginning of a program and continues through its completion. Therefore, students must be in frequent contact with their advisers. We accomplish this through the university Web community, e-mail, and informal meetings.

Evaluating the Portfolio

8. Have the students submit their portfolios for evaluation. A portfolio committee, three faculty members in our case, evaluates the student portfolios. We suggest setting a submission deadline of 3 weeks before the end of a program to allow portfolio committee members adequate time to thoroughly peruse the portfolios and make suggestions to students for revision. To evaluate the portfolios, each committee member uses a rubric we constructed based on our goals and objectives for each course as well as for the program itself.

9. Have the students showcase their portfolios in an interactive way. We hold a "portfolio party" with all students, portfolio committee members, and TESOL faculty members present. Computers are made available so students can display and share the original elements of their electronic portfolios with their fellow classmates and faculty.

Our teacher learners continue to use their portfolios even after they have finished their degree. Some have used their portfolios in job interviews. Administrators who view portfolios at the time of interviewing prospective teachers are enthusiastic about the opportunity to see actual materials they have developed and implemented, and have been impressed with the portfolios, as they give evidence of novel lesson plans and other curricular creations. Students have also commented that they plan to continue using their portfolios for their own professional development, collecting evidence of motivating and effective teaching strategies. In addition, our teacher learners recognize the benefits of portfolio assessment and are eager to employ the technical skills they acquire through this process of electronic portfolio evaluation. They have related that they plan to implement this type of evaluation in a modified form in their own classrooms.

Conclusion

The electronic portfolio has distinct advantages over other, more conventional forms of assessment, such as the traditional portfolio or comprehensive examination. Although lack of technological expertise was an initial barrier that we and our students had to hurdle, the assistance of our technology team and some well-spent time educating ourselves about how to incorporate technology in evaluation proved invaluable.

The electronic portfolio gives teacher learners the opportunity to demonstrate competencies developed during the course of study, serves as a reference for prospective employers, and augments their technological expertise, preparing them for the challenges of teaching diverse students in an increasingly high-tech classroom. Furthermore, teacher learners continue to use the portfolio for professional development and as a form of assessment for their own students. As one of our graduates put it, "I am convinced creating a portfolio is superior to traditional assessment; it is an opportunity to demonstrate my capabilities and creativity in the classroom."

As instructors at the university level, we have reflected on our experiences with the traditional comprehensive exam and realized that the use of electronic portfolios does more than just improve our assessment of teacher learners' work. In addition to being an innovative form of evaluation that is recommended in the literature, the portfolio has several advantages for graduate school instructors like ourselves. First, the creation of a portfolio reduces our students' anxiety about testing. Second, the implementation of portfolio assessment has the potential to bolster the university's reputation in preparing well-qualified teachers for the challenges of the ESOL classroom.

What is more, we came to realize that, although we as university instructors promote reflection in teacher education, we ourselves do not regularly take the opportunity to reflect on what we do in our instruction and why we do it. We were reminded that, although theory is extremely important in teacher education, praxis is what drives teaching. We therefore are resolved to practice what we teach by employing the authentic forms of evaluation we so vigorously endorse for our teacher learners, extending our professional contributions in the process.

Resources

Bullock, A. A., & Hawk, P. P. (2001). *Developing a teaching portfolio: A guide for preservice and practicing teachers.* Upper Saddle River, NJ: Prentice Hall.

The authors focus on preparing a teaching portfolio that can be used throughout the teaching career. Among other topics, they address the benefits of reflection, include a list of suggested components for the professional portfolio, and discuss the advantages of preparing an electronic portfolio.

Campbell, D. M., Cignetti, P. B., Melenyzer, B. J., Nettles, D. H., & Wyman, R. M., Jr. (1997). *How to develop a professional portfolio.* Needham Heights, MA: Allyn & Bacon.

This book describes step-by-step procedures for organizing a professional portfolio documenting the achievement of professional goals.

Campbell, D. M., Melenyzer, B. J., Nettles, D. H., & Wyman, R. M., Jr. (2000). *Portfolio and performance assessment in teacher education.* Needham Heights, MA: Allyn & Bacon.

Elements for designing a performance-based portfolio are described in this book.

Dodge, B., & March, T. (1995). *The WebQuest page.* Retrieved January 10, 2002, from http://edweb.sdsu.edu/webquest/webquest.html

This site provides a detailed description of the WebQuest concept and includes multiple links to sites that cover the whole process, from preparing a WebQuest to assessing student work.

Florida Education Standards Commission. (1996). *Preprofessional competencies for teachers of the twenty-first century.* Tallahassee, FL: Author.

McLaughlin, M., & Vogt, M. E. (1996). *Portfolios in teacher education.* Newark, DE: International Reading Association.

In addition to background information on portfolio assessment, the authors include a strong framework for designing and evaluating portfolios in university classes.

McLaughlin, M., Vogt, M. E., Anderson, J. A., DuMez, J., Peter, M. G., & Hunter, A. (1998). *Portfolio models: Reflections across the teaching profession.* Norwood, MA: Christopher Gordon.

This book presents the portfolio in three contexts: preservice teachers, teacher education, and in-service teachers.

National Board for Professional Teaching Standards. (2001). *English as a new language standards.* Arlington, VA: Author.

Rogers, G. M., & Williams, J. (1999). Building a better portfolio. *ASEE Prism, 8*(5), 30–32.

The article describes the implementation of an electronic portfolio in a preservice teacher context.

TESOL. (1997). *ESL standards for pre-K–12 students.* Alexandria, VA: Author.

Wilcox, B. L., & Tomei, L. A. (1999). *Professional portfolios for teachers: A guide for learners, experts and scholars.* Norwood, MA: Christopher Gordon.

The authors document the implementation of an electronic portfolio in a teacher education context. In addition, they explain the process of preparing a portfolio in various contexts: preservice teacher, in-service teacher, and teacher in a leadership position.

Contributors

Annis N. Shaver (ashaver@miami.edu), who has a BA in German and a BS in secondary education from Tennessee Technological University and an MA in German from Louisiana State University, is a doctoral student in TESOL at the University of Miami, in Coral Gables, Florida, in the United States. Having taught German and ESL in various locations in the United States and Germany, her primary interests lie in providing quality education to new teachers of ESL.

Juliet E. Hart (jhart@miami.edu) is a doctoral student in TESOL and special education at the University of Miami, in Coral Gables, Florida, in the United States. She has a BA in psychology and special education and an MSEd in TESOL from the University of Miami. Having taught diverse students with emotional disturbances for 6 years, her primary research interests include multicultural issues in special and ESL education.

Mary A. Avalos (mavalos@miami.edu) is a research assistant professor at the University of Miami, in Coral Gables, Florida, in the United States and is the director of the master's degree in TESOL scholarship program. She has a BS in multicultural studies from Concordia University, Irvine, an MA in educational administration/curriculum development, and a PhD in curriculum and instruction from the University of California, Riverside. Her primary research interests include literacy and educational issues in second language learning.

10 Thais That Bind: Becoming a Teacher Educator Through International Volunteering

Susan Carbery and Robert Croker

Narrative (Robert)

Phew! I had survived my first teacher education workshop! I was the leader of a cohesive and directed workshop in which everyone had fully participated in the activities that I had prepared. Why had I been so worried this morning? I just was not confident that my teaching experiences would be relevant to these teachers. Up to that point I had taught mostly Japanese high school students. How could teaching EFL in one of the richest countries in the world, where educational resources are seemingly limitless, possibly compare to teaching in an isolated Thai village? Here, there was a notable lack of the abundant audiotape players, photocopiers and copy paper, and computers found in most Japanese schools, and even an insufficient number of textbooks. However, from the very first day it was obvious that teachers, no matter where they are or what their situation is, have the same practical and immediate concerns: how to make their classes work and motivate their students to learn.

87

I looked around the lunch table that day after my first workshop session and caught Su's eye. She, too, clearly had the same sense of relief and accomplishment, and, above all, the feeling that we had connected with a completely different group of teachers from those she was used to working with in Japan. Moreover, the distinction between workshop leaders and teacher participants was not absolute. "I came here to help train teachers in EFL, but I think I may end up learning more than I teach," she confessed to me. I nodded in agreement. For us, the first day of that workshop in the sweltering Thai heat was to be the catalyst for the unfolding of our own professional development.

Su and I joined the CANHELP Thailand English Workshop Program in August 1998 to work as volunteer teacher educators in isolated primary and secondary schools in rural Thailand. It seemed a daunting prospect at the time but has been one of the most fulfilling experiences of our professional lives. Su had done some teacher development workshops before in Japan, but this was my first experience. We liked the idea of working in an entirely different context that would give us a glimpse of life on the other side of the fence. Doing something that was hands-on, that would allow us to work with teachers in their classrooms and in the workshop, was attractive. In addition, working in an organized program with other workshop leaders offered access to other teachers' knowledge, experience, and understanding. Su and I had looked forward to working in the rural Thai context but did not foresee how much it would benefit us. The workshops led to a productive, motivating process of reflecting on teaching practices, which ultimately improved our own classroom teaching. After 2 years as volunteer educators, we served as directors of the teacher education program also gave, an experience that allowed us to develop management and program coordination skills, expanded our perspective on teacher development, and inspired us to teach with renewed enthusiasm.

Description

The English Workshop Program we had joined was part of CANHELP Thailand, a Japan-based nongovernmental organization (NGO) aimed at promoting health and education for the children and adolescents of

Isaan, Thailand. Isaan incorporates the northeastern provinces of Thailand, bordering Laos and Cambodia. These provinces are the poorest and most arid in Thailand and do not benefit from the flow of tourist dollars, as do Chiang Mai in the northwest and the island provinces of the south. Although a very small component of CANHELP Thailand, the English Workshop Program is central to the concept of sustainable education. In Thailand, English language proficiency is one means of improving future economic prospects, as Thais proficient in foreign languages have more higher education and employment opportunities. From the beginning of our involvement with the English Workshop Program, we have felt that, no matter how many schools are built, books bought, and scholarships provided, the only effective way to sustain quality education and encourage its growth is to help educate the teachers.

In Isaan, teachers tend to be dispersed into small rural schools, with little opportunity for professional interaction. Therefore, the main aim of the English Workshop is to help teachers develop their capacity for greater control over their teaching environment; show them how to create lessons with minimal resources; and, most important, encourage them to share their ideas with other, equally professionally isolated teachers.

This program is now divided into three sections:

1. school visits: Volunteer teacher educators spend 2 days visiting village schools to orient themselves to the realities of education in that area, including meeting children and teaching some English classes.

2. English workshop: We conduct a 3-day workshop for English teachers from local primary schools and junior and senior high schools. We demonstrate active, interactive, and learner-centered activities, which we know are adaptable to most situations and teaching contexts. We also share effective classroom management strategies and brainstorm ways for teachers to create a relaxed yet active, learner-centered learning environment.

3. peer teaching seminar: With our oversight, the Thai teachers create an original student-centered activity based on a textbook unit and teach it to the rest of their group.

Steps

Becoming a teacher educator does not require anything more than the willingness to share ideas, energy, and creativity. Opportunities to do teacher education abound within your institution and local professional association meetings, at national and international professional association meetings, and under the auspices of international NGOs. You might seek out smaller, closer-to-home opportunities before spreading your wings wider, but as the narrative above shows, there are many paths to becoming a teacher educator.

Getting Started

1. Realize that you have much to offer to the professional development of other teachers. You do not need to be an experienced teacher educator. Merely sharing your teaching experiences and ideas with your peers can facilitate not only their professional development but also your own.

2. Collect successful activities. Keep a teaching log of what activities work for you and in which circumstances. Ask your colleagues what works well for them or how they approached the same activity, goal, text, or unit. Add these to your teaching log. When it comes time to prepare for the workshop, you can pick and choose from these activities.

3. Attend some peer presentations to get a feel for how the presenters conceptualize and package topics; what materials the presenters use; and how the presenters organize the materials, activities, and time. Also observe how the presenters present themselves, and make some notes on effective tactics and strategies.

Giving Your First Teacher Education Presentations

4. Give a minipresentation at work, or contact your local professional organization and offer to make a presentation. Professional organizations are often searching for presenters, and the atmosphere is usually relatively low key and the audience receptive to an energetic presentation.

5. Give the same presentation more than once. Repeating a presentation helps you tighten it, focus fully on its more critical aspects, and develop a larger set of activities, which in turn increases your flexibility.

6. Keep a presentation log. Before a presentation, one of us (Robert) makes a complete chart of ideas, activities, materials, and the time allocated to each. During the presentation, he makes notes on the chart about how the activities and materials worked and how to improve the presentation next time. Some presenters also make video recordings of their presentations.

Preparing for an International Workshop Program

7. Find an NGO whose goals, programs, and locations match your interests. Many NGOs have Web sites featuring previous volunteers' accounts, offering an accurate and realistic reflection of what your experience would be like. Contact the NGO, try to arrange to speak to previous volunteers, discuss your capacities and expectations, and select a program that matches your schedule and budget.

8. Read up on the area you are going to. Learn a little about the history and culture of the teachers you will be working with. Familiarize yourself with the teaching environment of the teachers who will be attending your workshop. Before doing the workshop, it is a good idea to visit some schools, chat with the teachers, and see a couple of classrooms in action. You will see not only what problems the teachers face in the way of classroom management and what methodology they are using but also what resources are available. If you cannot go to the schools before beginning to prepare your workshop, then talk to previous volunteers, or else contact the teachers by e-mail. Match your presentation to the teaching environment and the needs of the teachers.

9. If possible, ask for a copy of the textbook that teachers are using in their classrooms. Design your workshop around this textbook or the syllabus used by the teachers attending your workshop. You may even decide to demonstrate how to adapt or present particular lessons from the textbook for a particular

purpose. Often, all teachers need is inspiration on how to rework a textbook.

10. Decide on achievable goals for the workshop sessions. Do not be too ambitious: Concentrate on one theme or issue, such as how to adapt textbook activities into enjoyable, interactive, learner-centered activities or how to motivate students to communicate. Run your workshop plan past some colleagues or, even better, previous volunteers or the workshop coordinator.

Conducting the Workshop

11. As with the minipresentations and presentations, practice the workshop with your fellow volunteers. Arrange to get feedback from participants, and keep a presentation log, making notes during and after each presentation.

12. During the workshops, explicitly empower teachers to explore their teaching, experiment with new ideas, and be creative. Encourage teachers to take control, and remind them that they have the power to adapt and redesign any activity, be it the one you are demonstrating or any in their textbooks. Teachers often need to be reminded that making mistakes is part of any growth and development process.

13. Encourage teachers to reflect on their teaching and ask themselves why something did not work or why there is a problem in the classroom. An activity that did not work with one group of students may fly with a different group. Remind teachers not to abandon good activities or ideas without trying them out in different ways.

Following Up

14. Do not let your international volunteering end at one experience. Be prepared to continue volunteering for the same program or a different one. Not only will the programs benefit from the experienced volunteer educator you have now become, but you will continue to learn and develop personally and professionally. Recruit friends and colleagues, too.

15. If regular international volunteer education is not viable, consider organizing workshops closer to home. Share your ideas and activities with teaching friends and colleagues at your own school. You can even invite teachers from other schools in the district. Teacher education is both local and global.

Conclusion

After the first few years on the program together, we have taken different paths. The 2 years that followed exemplified how that initial volunteer experience changed and reinvigorated our professional lives. In 1999, the Thai government mandated a learner-centered approach to all levels of education in Thailand. As a result, one of us (Robert) created and directed six 3-day workshops in one Thai province, including one for nine Thai provincial educators, who continue to act as a resource. He now teaches secondary school teachers in Japan to use a learner-centered approach, through government and private programs. He has found that his teaching has continued to become more learner-centered through this experience, particularly as he went on to write his doctoral dissertation on the Thai program.

The other of us (Su) took over as the CANHELP Thailand English Workshop Program coordinator in 2000, not only changing, adapting, and developing the program into what it is today but also continuing to develop herself as a language educator and professional. She has also had the opportunity to consult on the EFL program at the secondary school attached to her university (Carbery & Sorrenti, 2001a, 2001b, 2001c).

Now, we have rejoined our talents, enthusiasm, and professional ideas and experiences. The next course on our professional journey is to create a sustainable teacher education network for teachers in developing countries, creating ties within the global teaching community through which teachers educate each other. For us, international volunteering has proved a fulfilling and practical way to reinvigorate our teaching and bind our global EFL profession closer together.

Resources

Beare, H. (2001). *Creating the future school*. London: Routledge Falmer.

CANHELP Thailand. http://www.canhelp.npo-jp.net

CANHELP Thailand is a Japan-based NGO that supports educational programs in the northeastern regions of Thailand.

Carbery, S., & Sorrenti, R. (2001a). A guide to instigating educational change: Four ways in which you can be part of the action. *The School House, 9*(2), 6–8. Retrieved December 17, 2002, from http://eslsv001.esl.sakuragaoka.ac.jp/tsh/9-2/9-2.pdf

Carbery, S., & Sorrenti, R. (2001b). A more professional approach to English education: The changes at Obirin High School. *The School House, 9*(3), 12–15. Retrieved December 17, 2002, from http://eslsv001.esl.sakuragaoka.ac.jp/tsh/9-3/9-3.pdf

Carbery, S., & Sorrenti, R. (2001c). Teacher action: Changing the system from within. In R. Long, K. Lane, M. Swanson, & G. van Troyer (Eds.), *On JALT 2000: Towards the new millennium* (pp. 38–45). Tokyo: Japan Association for Language Teaching.

Gebhard, J. G., & Oprandy, R. (1999). *Language teaching awareness: A guide to exploring beliefs and practices*. Cambridge: Cambridge University Press.

Global Citizens for Change. http://www.citizens4change.org

The site for this Canada-based organization describes opportunities for volunteering overseas.

High, J. (1993). *Second language learning through cooperative learning*. San Clemente, CA: Kagan Cooperative Learning.

Macaro, E. (1997). *Target language, collaborative learning and autonomy*. Clevedon, England: Multilingual Matters.

Nunan, D. (1988). *The learner-centered curriculum*. Cambridge: Cambridge University Press.

School for International Training English Language Fellow Program. (2002). Retrieved December 17, 2002, from http://www.sit.edu/elf

In this program, sponsored by the U.S. Department of State, U.S. citizens work overseas assisting language program development in developing countries.

Vikramshila Education Resource Society. http://www.vikramshila.org

Vikramshila is a teacher education organization based in India that aims to make quality education available to marginalized sectors of society.

Volunteer Educational Network. http://www.vol-ednet.com

> This Japan-based NGO aims to support teachers in economically disadvantaged regions, particularly Southeast Asia, by setting up networks and providing peer teaching workshops.

White, R. V. (1988). *The ELT curriculum: Design, innovation and management*. Oxford: Blackwell.

Wright, T. (1987). *Roles of teachers and learners*. Oxford: Oxford University Press.

Contributors

Susan Carbery (susan.carbery@wuc.ac.nz) is the director of studies/ program manager at Wollongong University College, in Auckland, New Zealand. She has an MEd in curriculum from the University of Southern Queensland and taught English in Japan for 11 years. She is the director of Volunteer Educational Network.

Robert Croker (croker@nanzan-u.ac.jp) is an associate instructor at Nanzan University, in Nagoya, Japan. His PhD, completed at Nagoya University, was based on his teacher education activities in Thailand. He continues to enjoy conducting teacher education workshops.

11 Starting a Local Teacher Study Group

Kazuyoshi Sato

Narrative

As a senior high school teacher in Japan a decade ago, I was in a dilemma as to how to teach English. I wanted to teach it as a means of communication by using authentic materials such as songs, movies, news broadcasts, and newspapers. However, I had to use boring textbooks to prepare students for university entrance examinations that put more emphasis on grammar knowledge and translation.

Fortunately, I met a group of teachers who had formed an informal study group. They encouraged me, and I became interested in innovative ways of teaching (see Sato, 2002b). I realized the importance of the study group outside the school as professional development. As a Japanese proverb warns, "Inonaka no kawazu" (a frog in the well does not know the ocean, or he that stays in the valley shall never get over the hill). I hoped to be in such learning communities and remain aware of alternatives throughout my career.

When I became a university teacher, I had the opportunity to create such a group. Communicative Language Teaching (CLT) *Kenkyukai* began in May 2000 as an informal study group for six teachers from the Nagoya area who wanted to share ideas. Besides benefiting as a teacher, as a researcher I could learn what was happening in classrooms and why implementing CLT was difficult in our context. Five more teachers joined after I introduced CLT *Kenkyukai* to participants in a 3-day workshop in August 2000. At this writing, 20 teachers—from universities, senior high schools (the majority of our participants), and junior high schools—have attended meetings.

How can a university researcher benefit from creating such groups? Study groups

- connect you to education as it is practiced daily in society and keep you from getting lost in the ivory tower
- provide data on language learning and teaching from the trenches
- allow you to serve the community, which can be gratifying when you receive reports of even small changes in the schools
- allow you to connect theory and practice and to explore novel ways of development
- keep you human, as they tie you to concerns that have no easy answers and dilemmas that force you to look more closely at the processes of education

Study groups build bonds between teachers who are isolated in their schools. Teachers learn by sharing their thoughts and ideas and discussing them openly. Professional meetings, however small or large or informal, are the changing grounds of the TESOL profession.

Description

The general goal of the CLT *Kenkyukai* is to improve our teaching by sharing ideas, materials, and teaching problems. More specifically, we wish to improve our practice by applying the concepts of CLT. Our monthly 2$\frac{1}{2}$-hour meeting includes a report on a textbook chapter that we have read in common, the sharing of risk logs, and discussions of teaching issues.

Our textbook report lasts about 1 hour. In 2002 we chose *Making Communicative Language Teaching Happen* (Lee & VanPatten, 1995) as our main source. In a typical meeting, the reporting teacher summarizes the main points of an assigned chapter and presents a couple of discussion questions.

For the rest of the meeting, participants share their risk logs, which are journals about teaching experience, and others comment. To create the risk log, each participant takes one small risk while teaching each month and writes about it (see Murphey, 2000, p. 108; see *CLT Kenkyukai*, n.d., for examples). Some teachers are too busy to keep a log and report orally instead. Ellis (1997) recommends microevaluation as one form of action research for teachers. Unlike a macroevaluation, which aims to evaluate a whole book or a whole set of materials, a microevaluation involves teachers in evaluating "the materials they use retrospectively on a day-by-day basis" (p. 230). Therefore, it helps them "examine and reconstruct their own pedagogical values and develop their own personal theories of language teaching" (p. 231). Accordingly, in our risk logs we record (a) what the activity was, (b) what the results were, (c) what we learned (our findings), and (d) how we might modify the activity (a possible solution).

Steps

The steps below are options to consider recursively rather than actual linear steps.

Getting Started

1. Start with a small group; keep it short and simple. CLT *Kenkyukai* started with six teachers: two colleagues from my old high school, three from other local schools, and me. Small and motivated is probably better than large and "along for the ride."

2. Give everyone the chance to talk. Let topics and format emerge naturally from the group's concerns and desires. At the first meeting, I talked about some of the issues of CLT and proposed

how the monthly meeting might be held. I stressed that all the participants would have equal opportunity to share their ideas and teaching problems. The meetings would not be run like formal workshops, which focus mainly on the transmission of good teaching techniques and knowledge.

3. Set goals and objectives. In the first few meetings and periodically afterward, we talked about teaching issues and decided on our goals. In our case, we found that almost none of the senor high school teachers had changed their teaching practice even though the Ministry of Education had instituted a new CLT syllabus in junior high schools in 1993 and senor high schools in 1994. For example, in many senior high schools the new subject Oral Communication often semiofficially became grammar lessons designed to prepare students for university entrance examinations. A couple of teachers confessed that they tried games and songs only once a month, when assistant native-English-speaking teachers visited their classes. Moreover, in their regular classes teachers focused mostly on translation and grammar, ignoring CLT principles. At the end of the first meeting, I had the participants fill out a questionnaire to find out their interests and teaching issues. They showed a keen interest in how to change their practices by incorporating innovative CLT ideas. In particular, they were concerned with how to increase the use of English (by both the teacher and the students in class), integrate language skills, and assess students communicatively.

Sustaining the Network

4. Create recursive means of open communication. After each meeting, I summarize the ideas presented in the meeting in a newsletter, which I send all the members by e-mail. I also advertise the date, time, venue, and main discussion topic of the next meeting to the group and more widely, and ask participants to spread the word.

5. Create an electronic discussion list. All the members have joined the list so that they can exchange ideas and support one another. For example, one member asked if anyone had

videotaped a television program about how famous Japanese athletes playing in foreign countries learned English. She got a response from one of the members immediately and received a copy of the video. Another member distributed a questionnaire for her MA thesis through the mailing list. Participants started to write to the list in English soon after a native-English-speaking teacher became a member in November 2001.

Expanding the Network

6. Create a Web page. I started to work on a Web page for CLT *Kenkyukai* (see Resources below) in summer 2000 to attract more participants. The site includes such pages as "What is CLT *Kenkyukai?*" "Next Meeting," and "Sharing Ideas." The site is also a place to collect in written form ideas that teachers presented in previous meetings. It is a humble site at present, but it is growing.

7. Organize a summer workshop. The first summer workshop for English teachers was held at my university for 3 days in 2001. The previous year, several new teachers had joined CLT *Kenkyukai* after I gave a summer workshop at another university I had taught at. I wanted to hold such a workshop at my own university as a way of attracting more teachers to the study group. I persuaded the administration that the workshop would be a good opportunity to advertise our university, and the university decided to support the program and to make it an annual event. For the theme of the workshop, I chose "How to Integrate Language Skills," because it was one of the main issues in our monthly meetings. A total of 36 teachers, mainly from high schools, participated, including 8 teachers from CLT *Kenkyukai*. Participants engaged in hands-on activities and shared their ideas and issues they face. In particular, teachers from CLT *Kenkyukai* told other participants what they had learned from the study group and how they implemented those ideas in their classes. At the end of the workshop I advertised CLT *Kenkyukai*. Knowing the limitations of short-term workshops, I hoped that the participants would join this continuous-learning group. Happily, one teacher came to the

following monthly meeting, and several teachers have subsequently joined our study group.

Extending the Learning

8. Take a study trip. We went on a 2-day study trip during spring vacation so that we could have a long discussion about our teaching issues. We set up the topic: how to integrate oral communication classes with regular English classes (reading, writing, and grammar). One senior high school teacher reported how she developed oral communication classes with her colleagues and showed videos on how her students improved their communication skills. Also, a new member, a native-English-speaking teacher, reported how he had been teaching oral communication class in his private junior high school, alluding to the difficulty of collaborating with Japanese English teachers. After the study trip, the native speaker sent an e-mail to the members:

> Just a quick message to say how much I enjoyed my first meeting with the English teachers' group. During the weekend I saw how much we all benefited from being around like-minded people. I just hope you get as much out of it as I do.

Conclusion

Those who participated in CLT *Kenkyukai* and the summer workshop are highly motivated teachers. Although not all members attend every meeting, the membership has increased from 6 to 20. The most difficult issue appears to be how to change the teaching culture each teacher belongs to and help teachers face the challenges these teaching cultures pose (see Fullan, 2001; Sato, 2002a). For instance, some members have invited colleagues from their schools to join CLT *Kenkyukai*, but so far only 2 teachers have joined. If teachers are more or less isolated in their schools, how can they share ideas they have learned from CLT *Kenkyukai* with their colleagues? In fact, a couple of teachers have complained that in their schools many teachers have given up trying out new ideas. They say most colleagues just hope to transfer to better public schools, not to face their present difficulties.

On the other hand, other teachers have been implementing new ideas little by little in their schools and have tried to communicate with other teachers. For example, in an English department meeting one senior high school teacher proposed incorporating a short essay into a term test. Her proposal was accepted, and she was able to motivate her students to write short essays in her class. Another senior high school teacher took advantage of the fact that she taught a third-year elective class of about 18 students, where she had the freedom to develop materials. She tried out recitation and speech contests, and found that her students gained confidence in using English.

I myself have benefited greatly from CLT *Kenkyukai*. I have found satisfaction in helping teachers who want to make a difference in their classes. Quite a few teachers have told me that they felt more supported in trying out innovative activities and giving them time to work. As a researcher, I have gained a better understanding of why CLT was (and still is) difficult and what kind of challenges teachers face in classrooms. I had the good fortune to become involved in a collaborative research project with one of the members (a high school teacher) with support from a local board of education. I became an adviser for a curriculum development project striving to create communication-oriented English teaching curricula. I hope such collaborative research will create a stronger community within the school and enrich CLT *Kenkyukai* as well.

In summary, CLT *Kenkyukai* is a continually evolving small community of inquiry and support, made up of teachers who might otherwise have been isolated in their working environments and who desire continual development. As one participant wrote,

> I have received many practical ideas from other teachers. I was encouraged by them and tried to use some of their ideas. Actually, I used half of the ideas soon after I went back to school, but had to modify the other half and saved them for later occasions. I have come to think that attending meetings and other workshops continuously is very important for my own growth as a teacher.

Resources

CLT Kenkyukai. (n.d.). Retrieved December 26, 2002, from http://www.nufs.ac.jp/~yoshi/pages/clt.dwt

The site includes a statement of the goals of CLT *Kenkyukai,* information about the next meeting, and a growing collection of several risk logs.

Fullan, M. G. (2001). *The new meaning of educational change* (3rd ed.). New York: Teacher's College Press.

Ellis, R. (1997). *SLA research and language teaching.* Oxford: Oxford University Press.

Ellis distinguishes between a macroevaluation and microevaluation by giving examples, and he recommends that teachers try the latter to develop their beliefs and practices.

Lee, J. F., & VanPatten, B. (1995). *Making communicative language teaching happen.* New York: McGraw-Hill.

Murphey, T. (2000). Becoming contributing professionals: Nonnative-English-speaking teachers in an EFL environment. In K. E. Johnson (Ed.), *Teacher education* (pp. 105–118). Alexandria, VA: TESOL.

Sato, K. (2002a). Practical understandings of communicative language teaching and teacher development. In S. J. Savignon (Ed.), *Interpreting communicative language teaching: Contexts and concerns in teacher education* (pp. 41–81). New Haven: Yale University Press.

Sato, K. (2002b). Seeking satisfaction. In K. E. Johnson & P. R. Golombek (Eds.), *Teachers' narrative inquiry as professional development* (pp. 150–162). Cambridge: Cambridge University Press.

Contributor

Kazuyoshi Sato (yoshi@nufs.ac.jp) teaches at Nagoya University of Foreign Studies, in Japan. He holds an MA and a PhD in applied linguistics from the University of Queensland in Australia. He has published several articles on communicative language teaching and teacher education. His current research interests include teacher development, teaching culture, and learning strategies.

12 Creating Publishing Communities

Tim Murphey, Mark Connolly,
Eton Churchill, John McLaughlin,
Susan L. Schwartz, and Jarek Krajka

Narrative

The five short narratives below seek to excite you about editing a variety of publications for your own and others' professional development. First, Tim proposes beginning with in-house newsletters to encourage students and staff to start engaging in professional conversations. Then Mark describes how an in-house journal can guide teachers through the research and writing stages. Eton and John relate their experiences co-editing a collection of working papers with the support of their community of qualitative researchers. Finally, Susan and Jarek describe the creation of their electronic journals, the first concerned with teacher education and the second with the use of technology in language teaching.

While all of these publications stimulate professional development in their contributors and readers, they also activate the professional development of those of us who have created and edit(ed) them. We hope our narratives will encourage you to think about producing the kind of publications that would work in your own professional communities. To guide you further, we finish with a brief description of publishing in the field, some general steps primed with questions, and a conclusion.

Starting Local Access Publications (Tim)

When I was a graduate student, one of my mentors was Pat Byrd, who at one point was editing three or four local and regional publications. I started off my writing career with descriptions of class activities. She published a few, and I got excited. Her newsletters and journals were very different from the seemingly insurmountable refereed, three-blind-copies, contact-you-in-4-months volumes I was assigned to read.

Later in my career, feeling somewhat lonely in academia and wanting to find like-minded explorers, I started my own local-access publication. I did it with my undergraduates in Switzerland, one of whom remarked, "I had always assumed that I had nothing worthy of saying or printing, and especially not in English! This makes me a real writer. I want to do more!" Later, at a university in Japan, I started *The Language Teacher Briefs*, which twice a year published short activity descriptions, essays, first-time book reviews, announcements, and small-scale research by students and teachers. At a university in Taiwan, I began *Exploring Learning* for students and teachers to contribute to, and I was an adviser for one group of students starting a student newsletter called *Cozy*. At the beginning, some material for these publications can come from student assignments to write book reviews or interview professors. Later, as in Switzerland and Japan, when students get excited about the publication, the assignments are not needed.

How do these experiences help me develop professionally? First, I can keep in touch with the fears and problems of would-be writers, and I enjoy seeing their confidence skyrocket when they see their names in print. Most importantly, though, publishing newsletters and journals that are accessible to all writers allows me to identify people who are interested in having the professional conversations that I crave. Hatch (1978) said, "Language learning evolves out of learning how to carry on conversations" (p. 404). My impression is that effective language teaching evolves in the same way. The pedagogical conversations in the process of writing, and later in print, are the lifeblood of our profession. They are the literacy acts that push us to improve, explore, and keep our eyes continuously open. I want to have as many of those conversations as I can, whether with beginning teachers or academic theoreticians. Creating local-access publications is one way to increase the number and quality of those conversations.

We know that writing things down helps reflection and cognition. However, TESOL professionals need to create nonthreatening opportunities within teachers' zones of possibilities if we want more professionals to get hooked on reflective teaching and professional conversations—and if we eventually want a larger and richer group contributing to the refereed, three-blind-copies, contact-you-in-4-months publications.

Writing With Teachers (Mark)

In my first year teaching EFL at a university in Japan, I learned I could advance my career only by accumulating academic publications. I had no such publications. I immediately joined my department's editorial committee, helped edit our in-house journal, and soon published my first humble article. That year, I recognized that my departmental colleagues, much like me, lacked experience with academic writing for publication or were anxious about it. The next year, I became editor-in-chief of the journal. I decided to use my position to help my colleagues and to learn more for myself about academic writing.

First, I researched and outlined six basic steps in planning and writing an academic article. I handed out reference materials on these steps to my colleagues and held help sessions on the topics. Next, I used the six steps as six deadlines for the annual journal, three deadlines roughly a month apart in spring term and three in the fall. I called it the Guaranteed Publication Program: My colleagues were guaranteed to have their articles published if they met all six deadlines with quality writing.

Here are the steps written in a form anyone can use.

1. research question or thesis statement: Write your topic in one succinct thesis statement or basic question your research is trying to answer. Narrow and define your topic.

2. references: Create an annotated bibliography. Locate your particular research niche in the broader field.

3. abstract, with working title: Write a one-paragraph summary of your research topic, and include a sentence or two about how you will conduct the research.

At this stage at least, or earlier preferably, you need to conduct some actual research. Though these steps make the process look linear, research and writing seldom are. They may be circular or jump around. You may discover interesting material in the teaching you have already been doing, for example, and then look for theories and background articles to support your work in writing up a research article. And because good writing means rewriting, three drafts are not a bad idea.

4. completed draft: Finish and write about all sections of the research. Find a colleague to edit this draft for organization and clarity.

5. rewritten draft: Using the feedback, rewrite the draft and submit it.

6. final draft: Incorporate suggestions for changes, minor or major, from editors and readers. Even if there are none, consider redrafting after a time, as your thoughts may have developed. If the paper is rejected, rewrite it using the recommendations and criticisms, and submit it to another publication. Keep it alive.

The six steps accomplished two main goals in our department. We published nearly double the number of articles as the previous year. Also, my colleagues had some basic guidelines to help organize their research and to complete their academic writing in a timely manner.

Through the editing process, I myself have gained the confidence to research, write, and publish. I have advanced my career by publishing more of my own articles, and I have discovered new research areas.

Co-Editing a Special Issue: Personal and Community Development (Eton and John)

Co-editing a special issue of an in-house volume in applied linguistics for Temple University Japan (TUJ) proved to be an excellent experience for us: We learned how to edit a scholarly volume and developed our community of qualitative researchers. In spring 2001, drawing from two of our existing communities, a study group at TUJ and our international mailing list, we recruited 12 contributors and began to foster a subcommunity of writers. We worked intensively with the authors during the summer to develop their papers, which were at various stages of readiness. The most valuable experience for us was learning to work as co-editors as we nurtured the work of our contributors. The best way to get a flavor of that experience is through the following composites of several messages that we exchanged in the late summer of 2001:

> Dear John,
> Your comments on Matt's autoethnographic piece are on the mark. I find it to be one of the most challenging to respond to because of the ethical questions that it presents. It is so good to have you as a co-editor (in addition to our peer editors) to be able to confirm and challenge my initial thoughts. I am finding myself stretched in so many ways by the project, not only in terms of the literature reviews in our peer papers, but also in terms of the process. Attached to this message, please find my comments to the papers by Kyoko and Rana. I hope my list of over 50 suggestions for corrections to Kyoko won't discourage her.
> Cheers,
> Eton
>
> Dear Eton,
> The editing process is indeed stretching us! I was shocked when I printed out your list of comments on Kyoko's paper. I had only been writing general comments in paragraph form to my contributors, but now I think that a numbered list is easier to respond to. I have already done two rounds of revisions with Rana, and I want to encourage her but it is frustrating not to see many revisions in mechanics, APA style, etc., particularly after the time I spent on giving her feedback. What do we do if a contributor hardly responds to our feedback? In the meantime, I have been doing so much editing lately that I don't know when I am going to find time to write my own paper!!!
> Regards,
> John

The messages above illustrate how both new writers and more seasoned contributors helped us learn the ropes of academic editing, even as we were assisting them with their revisions. We found the experience all the more rewarding because we could check with each other as we practiced our academic editing skills and received feedback from our contributors throughout the process. For example, one seasoned contributor told us that she had never learned so much from her editors before and that she had been amazed at our nurturing communications and guidance. Similarly, the gratitude of an author publishing for the first time helped us realize the importance of the community work that we were doing. We came to realize that good editing entails getting fascinated with writers about their subjects, providing them with quality feedback and resources, and communicating our belief in what they are doing. Every exchange like this not only pushes one along professionally but also constitutes the fiber that bonds the emerging community.

Teacher Training by Proxy: An E-Mail Journal (Susan)

In 1993, I became interested in publishing and, later, through jobs in Banjarmasin, Indonesia, and Nanjing, China, in teacher education. These interests coalesced into the creation of an electronic journal for teacher educators. I wanted to offer a resource to people who worked in places where it was not easy to obtain professional materials and to provide a place for people to publish their work.

It took about 6 months to create the first issue, which was published in 1998. First, I investigated whether an electronic journal devoted to teacher education already existed; none did. I decided to publish the journal via e-mail to make it as widely available as possible. I named it *Nexus: A Journal for Teachers in Development* to emphasize the link among educators that I wanted to create, and developed submission guidelines. I figured out formatting issues, developed a copyright policy, and decided the timing and frequency of publication. Getting an International Standard Serial Number (ISSN) lent credibility to the journal. Because the only cost to me is my time, subscriptions are free. The journal is not affiliated with any organization.

To solicit articles, I send announcements about *Nexus* to e-mail lists. Currently, I make all editorial decisions myself, although at some point I would like articles to be peer reviewed. Once articles have been accepted, I edit them and decide on a reasonable order in the journal. Each article usually goes through three drafts before the authors and I agree on a final version. Then I write an editorial introduction that mentions each article and connects all the articles to a common theme.

Finally, I send the journal to subscribers and announce on various e-mail discussion lists that *Nexus* has been published, inviting new subscribers. Whenever people request a subscription, I respond with a personal message thanking them for their interest. About 3 months after publication, which is about 4 months before the submission deadline, I send out announcements calling for submissions to the next issue.

Publishing an electronic journal is an incredible amount of work, but it is incredibly rewarding. I continue to learn something about teacher education from the articles, and I like to think that *Nexus* plays a small part in promoting the field of ESOL teacher education. That feeling of personal fulfillment and professional satisfaction when I see the finished issues of the journal makes it all worthwhile. (For information on submitting articles or subscribing, see the Resources section.)

Starting the E-Journal Teaching English With Technology (Jarek)

I developed a professional interest in the field of computer-assisted language learning (CALL) just a few years ago. I became a PhD candidate at Adam Mickiewicz University, Poland, and began work in the area of using the Internet to assist and supplement course book instruction, that is, using the Internet with a course book and as a course book. At the same time, I started passing on these ideas to teachers in courses I taught for the British Council Poland in cooperation with local teacher education centers, in-service teacher education programs, and publishers of English language teaching materials.

What bothered me when doing research for my PhD and running teacher education courses was the lack of a professional journal for EFL teachers dealing with technology. Those that existed were usually too academic and theoretical. They were not immediately useful for the average schoolteacher. There was a great need for a practical publication, written comprehensibly for schoolteachers and giving useful ideas and ready-made activities—a journal that would be willing to publish practical pieces, even single lesson plans. Fortunately, I found teachers who wanted to participate in such a journal by contributing Internet lesson plans, software reviews, or Web site reviews.

The initial aims of the journal, *Teaching English With Technology* (IATEFL Poland, 2002; see the Resources section), were to publish works in the field of CALL and to give teachers handy ideas applicable to the classroom, introducing technology and Internet-assisted learning. Furthermore, we wanted to stimulate participants in teacher education courses to read more about the field and to extend the knowledge and skills acquired during the course. Finally, we wanted to form an international community of teachers interested in computer-assisted teaching in order to raise the level of expertise. For teachers, a journal is not only a chance to publish their work and share their innovative ideas and approaches to teaching. It is also a way of sustaining their professionalism, getting them to think, and encouraging them to apply activities and ideas or adapt them to the reality of their classrooms.

We were fortunate to form an editorial team responsible for finding new subscribers, encouraging and reviewing contributions, and publishing new issues. Keeping the quality of publications high is important, and editors may sometimes face dilemmas. For example, do we publish low-quality material or have a shorter issue? The journal should also strive for objectivity, and the editors should follow ethical standards and procedures in the field. However, at the same time the journal needs funds to be published, and the way of funding the journal may sometimes affect its objectivity. The editorial team must somehow resolve all these issues, and the decisions are not always easy. Although it entails a lot of work, publishing a journal gives the satisfaction of answering the needs of an international community of teachers, transmitting new ideas, and encouraging individual teachers to become contributors and leaders in the field. And it is professional development *par excellence* for the editors.

Description

As shown by the narratives above, creating publishing communities in language education is a valuable networking activity. Many avenues are possible: newsletters by single classes and groups of teachers in an institution, in-house research publications, more broadly solicited research working papers, and e-mail and Web-based journals that span the globe. As forms of professional communication, these publications engender reflection first on the part of the creators/publishers and contributors and then on the part of the readers, potentially bringing them together in imagined communities (Norton, 2001) to enhance the practices of the profession. Such publications serve to unite groups small and large with their special interests and to encourage teacher development by inviting identification and continual learning. These publications are sparks igniting professional development activities far and wide.

Steps

1. Ask some general questions:
   - about the type of publication: What is the purpose? What is the focus? Who are the intended readers? Who are the potential writers? Who might be collaborators? Who might provide funding? On how small a scale can it start? What institutional resources, if any, could support the endeavor? What are the advantages and disadvantages of soliciting institutional support for the publication?
   - about editing: Do you have readers and collaborators to help with the editing? Could contributors act as peer reviewers to help with (and benefit from) the editing and reviewing process? What kinds of graphics could you use to make the publication attractive? How can you say no politely and positively when things do not fit? How can you develop tact when communicating with authors about their work? How do you decide on the layout of the publication?

- about the schedule: Working back from the publication date, when do you want the publication to be available? How much time does the printer or Webmaster need? How much time do you need to edit? When is the deadline for submissions? Is there a long enough time between the call for submissions and the submission deadline? If it is a serial publication, can you put a call and deadline into each issue?

2. Dive in, create a call for submissions, and send it out: Rarely will you have all the questions answered beforehand. It is the nature of publishing that many questions only present themselves during the process. In addition, the answers you have might shift with the production of your publication. Thus, flexibility is important, but being clear as to the purpose of the publication and clearly communicating the call for submissions will go a long way toward preserving your sanity and making the publication successful.

3. Edit, then monitor and adjust the submissions process: Are the instructions in the call for submissions clear and specific enough? Is the call reaching the intended audience? Are you getting the kinds of submissions you want? What can you do with what you are getting? How can you help your writers do a better job?

4. Edit, organize, and lay out: Put yourself in your potential reader's shoes and see how you might like the material ordered and laid out. Working with an editorial team at this point is reassuring.

5. Print or post (via e-mail or on the Web) and distribute: How will you get the publication to the target audience? Who needs to know it exists? How will you let people know?

6. Reflect on your processes of calling for submissions, editing, and dissemination: How can you make them easier and more efficient for the editors and better for the readers?

Conclusion

Although the work is daunting at times, publishing can be an extremely exciting and satisfying experience. Publishing professionally has allowed us to develop ourselves, create collaborative communities, help others develop (by writing, publishing, and reading), and contribute to the field. We look forward to seeing how others take on the challenge of publishing in the profession.

Resources

American Psychological Association. (2001). *Publication manual of the American Psychological Association* (5th ed.). Washington, DC: Author.

This edition is much more helpful than previous ones for citing electronic references but still is not particularly geared to qualitative research. The manual is widely accepted and used as a resource for academic writing. It includes sections on organizing a research article and presenting your ideas in writing, and contains vast details on style and usage. For online help with using APA style and citing electronic sources, see *APA Style* (http:// www.apastyle.org).

Denzin, N. K., & Lincoln, Y. S. (2000). *Handbook of qualitative research* (2nd ed.). Thousand Oaks, CA: Sage.

This edition is much more critical than the first edition and includes chapters on autoethnography (by Carolyn Ellis and Arthur Bochner) and testimonio (by John Beverly) that give helpful guidelines for qualitative research.

Hatch, E. M. (1978). Discourse analysis and second language acquisition. In E. M. Hatch (Ed.), *Second language acquisition: A book of readings* (pp. 401–435). Rowley, MA: Newbury House.

Insider Reports. (2002). *How to publish your own newsletter.* Retrieved December 28, 2002, from http://www.insiderreports.com/bizrprts /b8008.htm

Although this article is meant for entrepreneurs and businesses, the list of practical and survival-oriented tips and perspectives can be helpful for producing publications in education.

Lester, J. D. (1999). *Writing research papers: A complete guide* (9th ed.). New York: Longman. This resource book offers a range of advice on finding a topic, gathering data, organizing ideas, finding sources, taking notes, and writing up the research.

Murphey, T. (2000). Becoming contributing professionals: Nonnative-English-speaking teachers in an EFL environment. In Karen E. Johnson (Ed.), *Teacher education* (pp. 105–118). Alexandria, VA: TESOL.

Part of this article describes how access publications can be used with graduate students.

Newslink. (2003). *Education/campus magazines.* Retrieved January 17, 2003, from http://newslink.org/medu.html

This Web page lists links to education-related online magazines.

Newslink. (2003). *Internet magazines.* Retrieved January 17, 2003, from http://newslink.org/mcyb.html

This Web page lists links to online magazines on Internet-related topics.

Nexus: A Journal for Teachers in Development.

To subscribe or receive submission guidelines to *Nexus,* send an email message to slschwartz@earthlink.net with *Nexus: Subscription* or *Nexus: Guidelines* in the subject line.

Norris, J. (2002). *QualPage: Resources for qualitative research.* Retrieved January 17, 2003, from http://www.ualberta.ca/~jrnorris/qual.html

This Web page lists and categorizes resources for qualitative research.

Norton, B. (2001). Non-participation, imagined communities and the language classroom. In M. Breen (Ed.), *Learner contributions to language learning: New directions in research* (pp. 159–171). London: Pearson Education.

Publishing Business Group. (n.d.). *Magazine and newsletter publishing bookstore.* Retrieved January 17, 2003, from http://www.publishingbiz.com/html/bookstore.html

This Web page lists a series of books relevant to newsletter and magazine publishing with annotated descriptions to help you select those that are suitable for you.

Teaching English with technology. (2002). Retrieved January 16, 2003, from http://www.iatefl.org.pl/call/callnl.htm

Woodard, C. (2002). *Starting and running a successful newsletter or magazine.* Berkeley, CA: Nolo Press.

Woodward gives practical advice for newsletter and magazine publishers, including Web-based strategies.

Woodard, C. (n.d.). *How to make newsletters and magazines that will last.* Retrieved December 28, 2002, from http://www.publishingbiz.com/html/article_pub_success.htmlThis article gives six steps for creating a successful newsletter that are oriented toward business but useful for educators.

Contributors

Tim Murphey (mits@dokkyo.ac.jp) has studied and taught in Florida (MA), Switzerland (PhD), Taiwan, and Japan (where he now teaches at Dokkyo University). He is currently applying sociocultural theory to learning and teaching, teacher education, and alternative learning forms.

Mark Connolly (connolly_mark@hotmail.com) received his BA in creative writing and journalism from Fairhaven College and his MA in environmental politics from Western Washington University. He has been teaching EFL in the Center for English Language Education at Asia University, in Tokyo, Japan, since 1999, and for 2 years was editor-in-chief of the department's *CELE Journal.*

Eton Churchill (eton_c@yahoo.com) has taught languages in Japan and the United States at the secondary and tertiary level for over 15 years. He holds an EdD from Temple University Japan and currently teaches at Kanagawa University, in Yokohama, Japan.

John McLaughlin (jmcl@gol.com) taught EFL in Japan for 12 years at the high school and university levels. He is currently a doctoral candidate in education at Temple University Japan and a lecturer and research associate at the English Language Institute, University of Michigan, in the United States.

Susan L. Schwartz (slschwartz@earthlink.net) is an ESOL educator at Marsh Grammar School in Methuen, Massachusetts, in the United States, where she teaches students in Grades K–8 and helps educate teachers to work with English language learners. She has also worked in China, Indonesia, and other U.S. states as a teacher and teacher educator. Besides teacher education, her interests include materials development and making videos with her students.

Jarek Krajka (jkrajka@batory.plo.lublin.pl) works at the Department of Applied Linguistics of Maria Curie-Sklodowska University, in Lublin, Poland, where he teaches the methodology of teaching English and computer-assisted language learning. He is the editor-in-chief of the electronic journal *Teaching English With Technology* and a teacher educator for the British Council Poland Information and Communication Technology Project for Teachers.

Users' Guide to Strands in the Professional Development in Language Education Series

Chapters are categorized by their main strands only.

Administration and Organization _____

Collaborative Development for Teachers, Students, and Cultures _____

On the Move

Publishing

Volume 2

12 Creating Publishing Communities (Tim Murphey, Mark Connolly, Eton Churchill, John McLaughlin, Susan L. Schwartz, and Jarek Krajka; creating and editing accessible publications for teacher and researcher development)

Volume 3

5 Writing for Grant Dollar$ (Jane E. Averill)
6 The Roller Coaster Ride of Editing a Book (John M. Murphy)
7 Small Corrections: Becoming a Textbook Writer (Linda Grant)

Research and Presenting _____

Volume 1

3 In the Limelight: Presenting to Your Peers (Maureen Snow Andrade)

Volume 2

1 Long-Distance Collaboration: Rescuing Each Other From the Desert Island (Angela Beck and Joy Janzen)
4 Fostering Graduate School Teacher Development Through Peer Interviewing (Greta Gorsuch and David Beglar)
5 Pulp Fiction? The Research Journal and Professional Development (Simon Borg)

Volume 3

2 Becoming "Scholar of the College" (Andrew D. Cohen)
12 Sabbatical Projects Can Make a Difference: A Tale of Curriculum Revision (Sharon Seymour)

Teacher Education _____

Volume 2

10 Thais That Bind: Becoming a Teacher Educator Through International Volunteering (Susan Carbery and Robert Croker)
11 Starting a Local Teacher Study Group (Kazuyoshi Sato)

Volunteerism, Advocacy, and Politics _____

Also Available From TESOL

Academic Writing Programs
Ilona Leki, Editor

Action Research
Julian Edge, Editor

Bilingual Education
Donna Christian and Fred Genesee, Editors

Community Partnerships
Elsa Auerbach, Editor

Content-Based Instruction in Higher Education Settings
JoAnn Crandall and Dorit Kaufman, Editors

Distance-Learning Programs
Lynn E. Henrichsen, Editor

Grammar Teaching in Teacher Education
Dilin Liu and Peter Master, Editors

Implementing the ESL Standards for Pre-K–12 Students
Through Teacher Education
Marguerite Ann Snow, Editor

Integrating the ESL Standards Into Classroom Practice:
Grades Pre-K–2
Betty Ansin Smallwood, Editor

Integrating the ESL Standards Into Classroom Practice:
Grades 3–5
Katharine Davies Samway, Editor

Integrating the ESL Standards Into Classroom Practice:
Grades 6–8
Suzanne Irujo, Editor

125

Integrating the ESL Standards Into Classroom Practice:
Grades 9–12
Barbara Agor, Editor

Intensive English Programs in Postsecondary Settings
Nicholas Dimmitt and Maria Dantas-Whitney, Editors

Interaction and Language Learning
Jill Burton and Charles Clennell, Editors

Internet for English Teaching
Mark Warschauer, Heidi Shetzer, and Christine Meloni

Journal Writing
Jill Burton and Michael Carroll, Editors

Mainstreaming
Effie Papatzikou Cochran

PACE Yourself: A Handbook for ESL Tutors
Teresa S. Dalle and Laurel J. Young

Teacher Education
Karen E. Johnson, Editor

Technology-Enhanced Learning Environments
Elizabeth Hanson-Smith, Editor

For more information, contact
Teachers of English to Speakers of Other Languages, Inc.
700 South Washington Street, Suite 200
Alexandria, Virginia 22314 USA
Tel 703-836-0774 • Fax 703-836-6447 • publications@tesol.org
• http://www.tesol.org/

T E S O L